ALGONQUIAN AND IROQUOIS
CRAFTS FOR YOU TO MAKE

Messner Books by Janet & Alex D'Amato

Algonquian & Iroquois Crafts For You To Make
African Animals Through African Eyes
African Crafts For You To Make
Colonial Crafts For You To Make
More Colonial Crafts For You To Make

ALGONQUIAN AND IROQUOIS

CRAFTS FOR YOU TO MAKE

Janet and Alex D'Amato

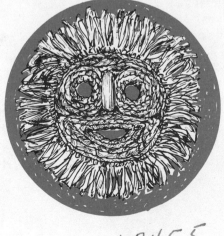

JULIAN MESSNER   NEW YORK

Published by Julian Messner, a Simon & Schuster
Division of Gulf & Western Corporation, Simon &
Schuster Building, 1230 Avenue of the Americas,
New York, N.Y. 10020.

Manufactured in the United States of America

Design by Janet & Alex D'Amato

Second Printing, 1981

Library of Congress Cataloging in Publication Data

D'Amato, Janet.
  Algonquian & Iroquois crafts for you to make.

  SUMMARY: Suggested craft projects accompany a
discussion of the life and customs of the Algonquian
and Iroquois Indians.
  1. Indian craft—Juvenile literature. 2. Algonquian
Indians—Social life and customs—Juvenile literature.
3. Iroquois Indians—Social life and customs—Juvenile
literature. [1. Indian craft. 2. Algonquian Indians
—Social life and customs. 3. Iroquois Indians—Social
life and customs. 4. Handicraft. 5. Indians of
North America—Social life and customs] I. D'Amato,
Alex, joint author. II. Title.

TT22.D35   745.5   79-15487
ISBN 0-671-32979-0

*Shown on the title page: a fetish,
model of Iroquois house, a
Wampum belt and husk face mask*

*On this page: Iroquois mask
Opposite: Underwater panther
motif on a woven bag
(Algonquian)*

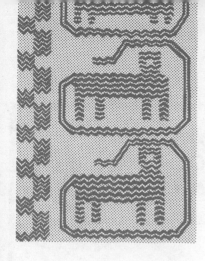

CONTENTS

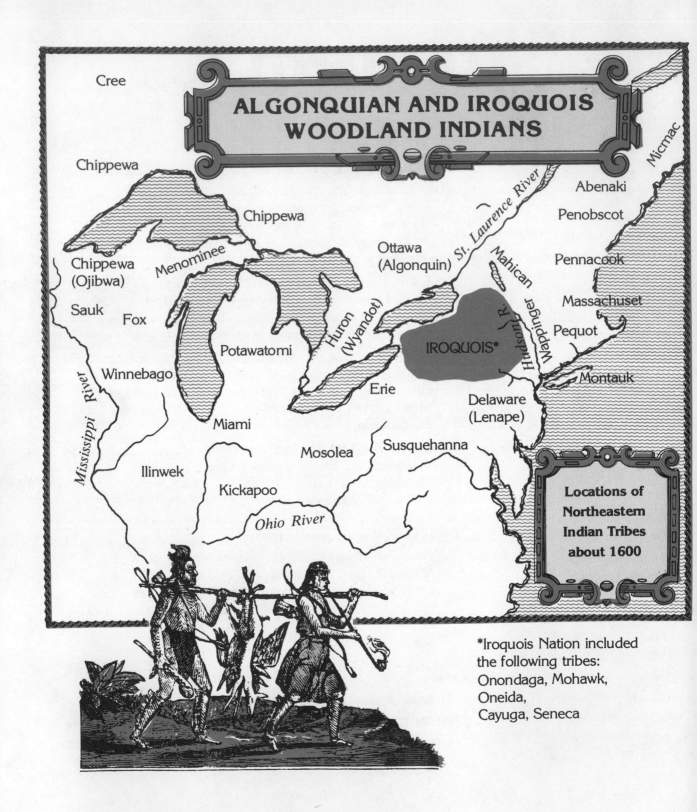

ALGONQUIAN AND IROQUOIS WOODLAND INDIANS

Cree

Chippewa

Chippewa

Chippewa
(Ojibwa)

Menominee

Sauk

Fox

Potawatomi

Winnebago

Miami

Ilinwek

Kickapoo

Ottawa
(Algonquin)

St. Laurence River

Huron
(Wyandot)

Erie

Mosolea

Ohio River

Mississippi River

Micmac

Abenaki

Penobscot

Pennacook

Massachuset

Mahican

Hudson River

IROQUOIS*

Wappinger

Pequot

Montauk

Delaware
(Lenape)

Susquehanna

Locations of Northeastern Indian Tribes about 1600

*Iroquois Nation included the following tribes: Onondaga, Mohawk, Oneida, Cayuga, Seneca

INTRODUCTION

For thousands of years the woodlands from the Atlantic Ocean to the Mississippi provided a home for wandering hunters, the people whom Europeans later called Indians. They hunted the game and fished the numerous rivers, gradually banding together in small groups, then into larger groups or tribes. Some tribes began to roam less, settling in certain areas for long periods of time.

The woodlands could be an excellent provider; there were trees for making homes, durable bark for containers, game to provide both food and clothing. Everything necessary for survival was gathered from the earth and forests—but not easily. Much knowledge, hard work and skill were needed. Bark, trees, vines and reeds were used for making shelters. The weather could be harsh, the food supplies uncertain. They found plants they could eat and others to use for medicine. Some tribes learned to cultivate a few vegetables in summer, then moved on to winter hunting grounds. Gradually, they learned to preserve some foods.

These early tribes inhabited the northeastern woodlands for many centuries. Each tribe spoke a different language, yet many speech and living patterns were similar, indicating common origins. These tribes collectively have come to be called Algonquians.

Sometime after A.D. 800 another group of tribes began to invade the Algonquians' area. It is believed they came up from the south. These invaders pushed into lands south of Lake Ontario, and east towards the Hudson River, displacing the tribes living there. The new tribes (solid color on the map) were farmers as well as hunters. They brought corn, which was not native to the woodlands area, and began to cultivate it along with other vegetables.

There was constant warfare between the invaders and the Algonquians, as well as fighting among their own tribes. Finally, the invaders realized they could combat their enemies more effectively if they united. Around 1570, five tribes: Mohawk, Onondaga, Oneida, Seneca and Cayuga, joined together to form the

Iroquois Nation, also called the Five Nations. Councils of the Five Nations resolved differences and made treaties which stopped fighting among member tribes. They created a workable and effective governing system. Later other tribes joined them.

Around the Iroquois Nation were the Algonquian tribes. Lenape (later called Delawares) lived to the east and south. North and east, in the New England area were many tribes, among them the Pequot and Penobscot. To the west, north of the Ohio River, were other Algonquian tribes, such as the Chippewa around the Great Lakes.

The Five Nations was at the height of its power when Europeans arrived. In time, both Algonquians and Iroquois began absorbing European ways. The Indians traded furs, which were in much demand in Europe, for various goods to make their lives easier. When steel replaced the stone axe and knife, cutting a tree, or skinning and cutting meat, became easier. Iron kettles for cooking and fabric for clothing were conveniences the Indians had not had before the Europeans came.

But the Europeans also brought diseases, liquor and guns. The Indians had no immunity against diseases such as smallpox, typhoid, and measles, and many died. And while guns made hunting easier, they also made warfare deadlier.

Most Algonquian tribes were friendly at first, and showed European settlers how to live on the land. The Iroquois were less friendly. They recognized the value of trade, but had well-organized resistance against any Europeans—and there were many—who cheated in trade or infringed on Iroquois lands or customs.

The crafts of the woodland Indians soon became a blend of native and European materials and styles. Most Indians had excellent design sense and great skill working with difficult materials. Ceremonial items were carefully decorated with significant designs. Religious beliefs were part of all the Indians did and made. Some household goods were ornamented, but little was ever made for decorative purposes only. Art was part of everyday life, not something separate.

Indian skills are an important part of the heritage of this country. You can enjoy just reading about them, or you can go on to make something that may derive its inspiration from an Indian motif or technique, keeping the crafts tradition alive.

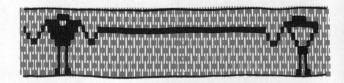

Wampum Design

MATERIALS AND METHODS

The Indians used great ingenuity with the materials they had available to them. Few of us today could really work with these materials. The early Indians used things they found around them, and wasted nothing. You should do the same. Most of the projects in this book call for modern-day materials such as plastics, but alternate suggestions for using more authentic materials are also made.

Before starting any project, read it through completely so you'll know what you will be doing. Gather up the materials and tools needed. Many of the things you will need can be found around the house. Other things can be bought at local variety, hardware or sporting goods stores. Materials like raffia and feathers can be purchased from craft suppliers. There is a list in the back of the book.

Tools

The Indians originally used stone tools, tediously chipped to make a sharp blade. Metal tools from Europe made cutting and drilling easier.

A few basic tools you may need are shown here. Most are available at any hardware or discount store if you should need to buy any.

All tools should be used carefully, with adult supervision.

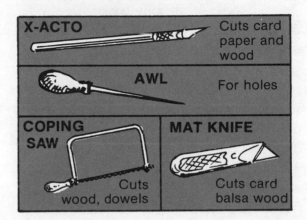

X-ACTO	Cuts card paper and wood
AWL	For holes
COPING SAW — Cuts wood, dowels	MAT KNIFE — Cuts card balsa wood

Materials

Materials do not have to be new. Often at rummage or garage sales you can find beads, fabric, felt or other craft materials. Use your imagination when reading the materials listed at the beginning of each project. You may think of other sources of materials than those given.

Fur and leather: Buy fake fur at a fabric store, when "Fur" is suggested. Or you might find some scraps of real or fake fur at second hand sales. Chamois used for cleaning cars is a useful, workable leather. Heavier leather might be found second-hand—an old bag, vest or mini-skirt. Or buy leather in a craft store.

Raffia: is a natural product. There are also imitations available called Swisstraw, Strawtex, or Ribbon Straw. Most imitation raffias have a shiny look, but Swisstraw now makes a mat or dull finish which looks more like the real thing.

Reed: for making baskets is also a natural product. A plastic imitation is available and both kinds are sold in craft stores.

Wood: Use natural sticks and bark if you have access to woodlands. Just make sure you only remove pieces that are dead and fallen on the ground. *Never* cut, peel or otherwise injure a living tree. If wood must be purchased, buy dowels or balsa wood in craft store. Dowels come in various sizes. Balsa wood is easily cut and shaped.

Cardboard: is suggested as a substitute for bark. Heavy card can be cut from side of a corrugated shipping carton, usually available from supermarkets. For lightweight card, use oaktag bought in stationery or art stores, or the backs of writing pads or shirt boards. Pressed card trays in which produce or eggs are often packed are another source of card. Cut lightweight card with scissors. A knife may be needed for the corrugated card.

Glues: The Indians did not use glue. Instead, they depended on well-tied joints, or sewing, to hold things together. For you, glue is best to make models and other crafts. White glue such as Elmers or Sobo will do for most purposes. Sobo is best for fabric and holds on Styrofoam. To join hard surfaces such as metals, use household cement (Duco). To hold pieces together while drying, use clips—either clip clothespins or stationery clips (Fig. 1).

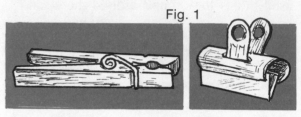

Fig. 1

For large areas, or soaking paper strips, use wallpaper paste. Mix in a container, then let set. If too thick, add water until quite thin. Cover container and use as needed.

To build up small areas, a maché pulp sold in craft stores called Celluclay is useful. Mix as directed on the package.

Paints and Stains: The Indians used certain berries, nuts, roots and barks to supply colored pigments. Other paints were made of colored earths or powdered rocks mixed with bear or other fat. By 1870, when dyes were commercially available, the Indians usually preferred them to the tedious processing of natural colors. Today, many paints are available. Acrylic or household latex can be thinned with water, but will be waterproof once it dries. Wash brushes with water immediately after using. Watercolor or poster paints can also be used for most purposes.

Small areas of color can be added with felt-tip markers. To imitate beadwork, dab markers straight down (Fig. 2), making design of dots of colors.

When using paints or other messy materials, wear a smock and cover working surface with newspapers.

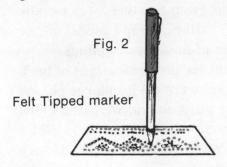

Fig. 2

Felt Tipped marker

Sewing

It was a difficult process sewing with sinew through holes punched in leather. When thread, metal needles and fabric could be obtained, sewing became easier for the Indians. Today, a great variety of fabrics and sewing supplies can be purchased. Most stores carry decorative embroidered tapes (Fig. 3) with Indian-type designs.

Fig. 3

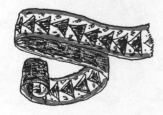

To sew, use long stitches for basting or gathering (Fig. 4). Make smaller stitches, close together, for seams (Fig. 5). Use backstitch for a sturdier seam (Fig. 6) or overcast (Fig. 7). To sew an overlap seam, insert needle as shown (Fig. 8). The couching stitch needed for beading and embroidery is shown on page 64.

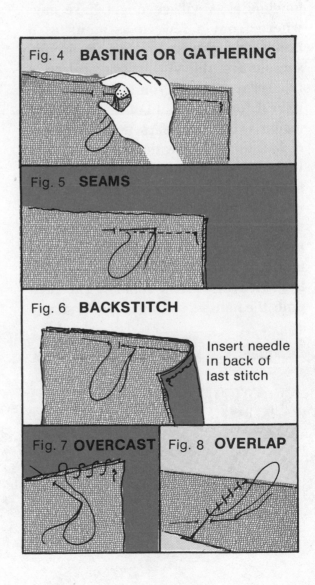

Fig. 4 **BASTING OR GATHERING**

Fig. 5 **SEAMS**

Fig. 6 **BACKSTITCH**

Insert needle in back of last stitch

Fig. 7 **OVERCAST**   Fig. 8 **OVERLAP**

1 HOUSES

The Iroquois lived together in groups of five to fifteen families in a longhouse. A village might have anywhere from a few to as many as a hundred longhouses. A stockade usually surrounded the village for protection from enemies. Beyond the stockade were fields of corn and other vegetables. About every ten years the village was moved to a new location. By then crops were poor, the soil giving out, and the longhouses were beginning to rot.

Iroquois houses belonged to the women. When a daughter married, her husband came to live in her family's house. When a son married, he went to live with his wife's family. The men built the houses, setting a row of sturdy poles along the outside edge and another row inside. Young boys, who weighed less than the men, climbed the framework to lash on the upper crosspieces making the framework. Lashing, or tying together, was usually done with withes, strips made of the inner layer of basswood saplings.

To cover the house, slabs of bark (usually elm) were cut into large pieces. Slabs were piled up and weighted down so they would flatten and dry. Holes were then punched in the slabs and they were strung together, set against the framework, and tied on in rows. Poles placed on the outside were tied through holes to inner poles to hold the slabs in place.

Iroquois Village showing Longhouses

Algonquians made a smaller home, or wigwam, usually for one family. A larger structure was used for gatherings and ceremonies. Some tribes, such as the Chippewa, who moved about to get their food, needed housing at various locations. They made their winter homes in a sheltered wood. Hunting was better there and the trees gave some protection against the severe winters. In spring they traveled to an area where they would spend several weeks gathering maple suger. Their summer home was in an open area where they could plant crops. For each move they carried house coverings and possessions, usually by canoe. By fall they moved to the marshes to gather wild rice.

For the house framework, saplings were set in a circle or oval, bent, and lashed over the top. The framework was left in place for reuse the next season.

Framework sides were covered with rush mats made of cattails or woven grasses. In areas where birchbark was plentiful, the top was covered with strips sewn together and sticks lashed to each end. Birchbark strips could be rolled up and carried with them. Sometimes the entire frame was covered with mats. In winter, houses had extra layers of mats and bark.

Wigwams
(Algonquian)

Summer homes were similar, with less covering, and often a porch was added where women and girls spent much time at their work.

For temporary shelter, some tribes made cone-shaped dwellings. The Delaware and most New England tribes made round, dome-type houses covered with heavy bark. Used year-round, some combined the round top with a multifamily structure making long units.

Instructions follow for making a model of a longhouse and wigwam. The structure will be more easily understood after you make one. Variations can be made. For instance, a Delaware or New England house might be wigwam-shaped but covered with slabs of elm bark like the longhouse. Northern New England Indians used birchbark in a similar manner to those of the Great Lakes region.

MODEL HOUSES

Longhouse (Iroquois)

(See house on Title Page)

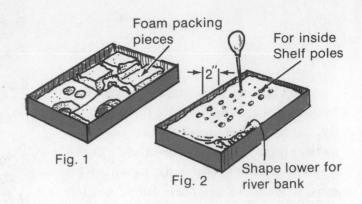

Foam packing pieces

For inside Shelf poles

Fig. 1

Fig. 2

Shape lower for river bank

MATERIALS: Styrofoam, corrugated box, reed (used for basket making), thin sticks about 1/16″ diameter, tan and brown crepe paper, brown wrapping paper or bags, thin cardboard, produce tray from supermarket (maché type), buttonhole thread needle, Sobo glue, wallpaper paste, newspapers, clip clothespins, awl.

For base, use a piece of Styrofoam 12″ x 14″ x 1″ or larger. Or use discarded foam packing for appliances, cut and shaped. Place oddly shaped pieces in a corrugated carton cut down to about 2″ high (Fig. 1). Arrange, creating some level surfaces. Fill gaps with torn, crumpled newspapers. Tear strips of thin brown paper bags—not heavy supermarket bags. Soak in wallpaper paste. Cover surface with strips making a fairly level ground. Add a final layer of brown crepe paper, if desired. One corner could be shaped lower to look like a river bank (Fig. 2). If using a slab of Styrofoam, spread on thinned Sobo and cover with a single layer of brown paper or crepe paper, covering edges.

Determine size of house. A longhouse was about as high as wide, usually 15 to 20 feet. Length varied. For instance, a model 5″ high, 5″ wide and 10″ long would be in scale of a house 30 or 40 feet long.

Plan to locate house on the base so there will be area around the house on one side and one end. Mark the base with area for the house. With an awl, poke holes about 2″ apart for placing poles. For inside shelves, make another row of holes (Fig. 2) 1″ or 1½″ in (about 1/4 of width).

As shown, cut a piece of cardboard for a guide (Fig. 3). Soak reeds in water. Cut two pieces about 1/4″ longer than the measurement determined in Fig. 3. Place reeds in first set of holes and curve over to meet at the top. If length is correct, they should overlap enough to tie together. Cut enough pieces for outside row of holes. Put a dab of glue in each hole, insert reed end, and allow to dry.

To tie at the top, get a partner; one holds the reeds together in position, the

Fig. 3

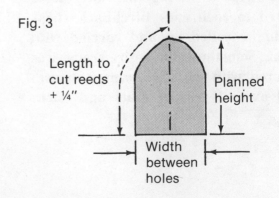

Length to cut reeds + ¼″

Planned height

Width between holes

other ties. Hold the card guide below to establish uniform height. Cut a piece of thread or string, add a dab of glue, and tie the reeds together at the top (Fig. 4).

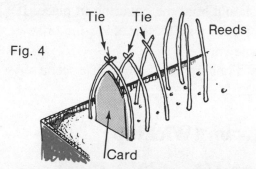

Fig. 4

Rigid sticks are best for the inside structure; use wooden skewer sticks, or reeds from an old matchstick curtain or place mat. However, reeds could be used if none of these are available. For inside verticals, measure from hole to roof, add 1/4″ (Fig. 5). Cut sticks to size, put glue on tip of each vertical, and push into holes. Tie or glue sticks to reeds where they touch at the top. Hold together with clip clothespins until glue dries.

For horizontals, measure and cut eight sticks, each the length of the house. Position and tie to the inside of vertical sticks (Fig. 6). Tie at ends; glue other intersections as needed. Allow glue to dry.

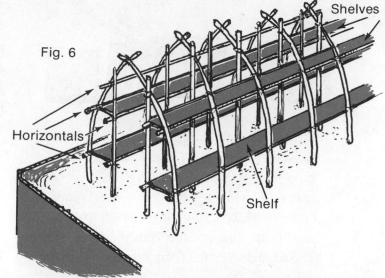

Fig. 6

These will hold the storage shelves. Cut two more sticks; glue and tie above the shelves.

Make the bed and storage shelves. Measure and cut four cardboard pieces to fit onto the horizontals. Glue a layer of tan crepe paper on each piece. Glue the cardboard to horizontals (Fig. 6).

Measure, cut, and glue short reeds to the ends of the house (Fig. 7), leaving a door on each end.

For covering, cut flat sections from maché trays or tops of egg cartons. Spread wallpaper paste on each surface. Lay on brown crepe paper and press down with wet fingers, pushing it about a bit to get a lumpy bark look. When dry, cut into

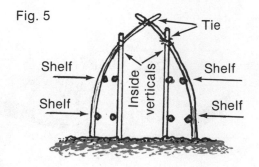

Fig. 5

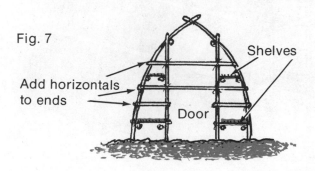

Fig. 7

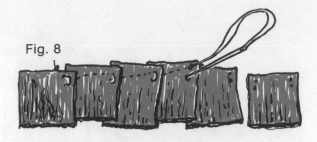

Fig. 8

squares slightly larger than the distance between uprights. Thread needle, push through corner of square (Fig. 8) into next square, sewing together and overlapping slightly. Make a row long enough to cover length of framework. Cut pieces to fit around and over the door at one end. Glue and tie in place.

To cover side, set the first row of slabs against the house at ground level. Place the next row above, slightly overlapping, tie at ends, and glue securely to frame. Hold with clips until glue dries. Then do next row. Continue until one side is covered. Leave the other side open so the inner structure can be seen. At top, cut individual pieces to fit. Fold over ridge, glue, and sew on. For smoke holes, leave openings at intervals (Fig. 9). Cut more reeds, slightly longer than first set. Poke

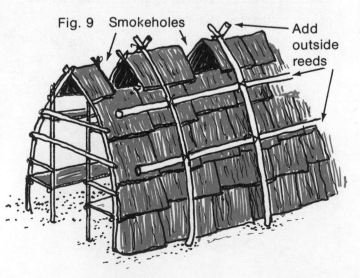

Fig. 9   Smokeholes

Add outside reeds

holes in base along outside edges; insert end. Bend over covering; tie at the top. Add two or more horizontals and slide behind the outside vertical sticks (Fig. 9). This should hold the covering in place. If some pieces tend to slip, add glue or sew to framework.

For completed longhouse scene see page 22.

For completed longhouse scene see page 22.

Wigwam (Wickiup)

MATERIALS: Similar to longhouse, plus: corn husks, white crepe paper, brown or black felt-tipped markers.

Make a base as suggested for longhouse. This time, plan a circle or oval area. The average house was about 16′ x 20′ x 8′ high, the height being about half the width. Decide on the size to best fit your base and draw on oval or circle. For instance, plan an oval 8″ x 10″ and 5″ high. Poke in holes about 1½″ apart. Cut a piece of reed, curve it over to determine the size needed for the highest point. Cut two this size. Cut two more pieces of reed, slightly shorter (Fig. 10), then cut two more slightly shorter, to create the dome shape. Make two curved pieces across, up

Fig. 10

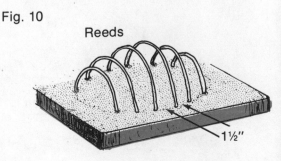

Reeds

1½″

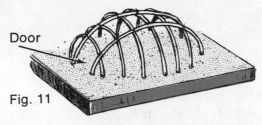

Door

Fig. 11

and over from the door to the opposite side (Fig. 11). Determine size, trim reeds and reposition. Push reeds deeper into base or pull up slightly to make a dome shape. When a satisfactory shape is established, add glue to tips and insert into base the proper depth. Glue and tie at intersections where needed. Allow to dry.

Glue and tie on three horizontals around house (Fig. 12). Leave area on one end open for door. If possible, make door opening large enough to get your hand inside the house to make it easier to attach coverings.

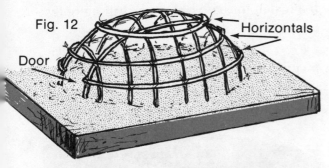

Fig. 12

Horizontals

Door

This house also had bed and storage shelves. Cut and place upright, vertical sticks (Fig. 13) and horizontals. Attach

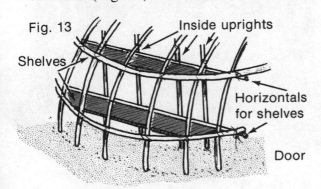

Fig. 13

Inside uprights

Shelves

Horizontals for shelves

Door

as for longhouse (see Fig. 5 & 6). Determine size needed for shelves. Cut out of card and cover with brown crepe paper or corn husks. Glue in position (Fig. 13).

For the summer house, add the outside platform. Cut two rigid sticks about the same height as the house. Poke holes approximately 2″ away from one side of the house. Add glue and insert vertical poles (Fig. 14). Measure and cut sticks for crosspieces. Tie and glue to frame as shown. For platform shelf, measure and cut a cardboard shape to fit onto horizontals; attach in position.

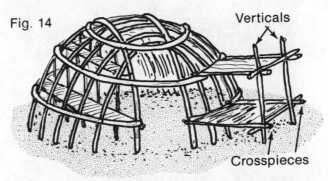

Fig. 14

Verticals

Crosspieces

For the look of mats to cover the lower part of the frame, use corn husks. Select wider pieces, if possible, and dry in the sun. Work with husks slightly damp. Trim ends. Cut in pieces to cover at least halfway up the frame. Cut a piece of reed to attach around the outside of the house to hold the coverings. Thread a needle; use double thread. Tie the end to inner reed. Sew out, then push needle back through husk piece. Reach inside doorway to get

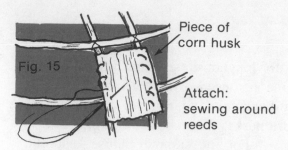

Fig. 15

Piece of corn husk

Attach: sewing around reeds

needle and push out again (Fig. 15). Also place and sew around outside a reed (Fig. 16). It is easier if you have a helper holding the piece while you sew. Cover lower half of house, base row first, adding pieces of husk as needed. Add glue to framework to help hold if needed. Glue and sew on husk pieces to make porch roof.

Fig. 16

Outside reed

For the birchbark look on top, glue or paste white crepe paper on brown paper. When dry, cut in strips. With dark marker, dab on spots to look like birchbark. Draw on lines and stitching to indicate the way the Indians sewed the bark pieces together (Fig. 17). Glue a small stick on each end. Lay across the top, leaving open area for smoke hole. Glue and sew in place as needed (Fig. 18).

Fig. 17

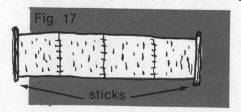

sticks

ALTERNATES: Real bark makes a more authentic look for Iroquois house, if you can find a fallen log such as cherry or dark birch with thin bark that peels off easily. Wash and clean bark thoroughly and, as a precaution, spray with bug spray. When dry, cut and add as shown (Fig. 8–9). Real white birch could top the wigwam, but remove only pieces from fallen limbs, never a living tree.

To make the base look like real ground, before making house cover the base with layers of soaked paper and then sprinkle sand over the wet paste. When dry, shake off excess.

For a group project, make a larger model. It's easier to work. Use industrial foam slab for base or wood, drilling holes as needed.

If you should have a large calendar picture or a small poster showing a woodland scene, mount it on card and attach at back to create a diorama look.(Fig. 18).

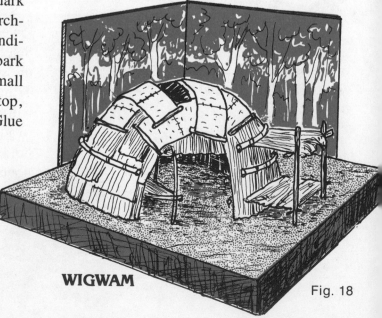

WIGWAM

Fig. 18

18

IN AND AROUND THE HOUSE

The woodland Indian spent much time outside. Inside, areas to live and store their belongings were very limited. The top shelves of the house were used for storage of food and possessions. Sometimes a child slept there. The bottom shelf was the bed or seating for the entire family. Under the bed shelf, more goods were stored: baskets, utensils, rolls of leather ready to be made into clothing. Strips of pumpkin, strings of corn, dried fish, as well as other possessions, such as a quiver of arrows and bow, hung from the inside poles.

In the longhouse, the fire served two families. Each family had a space about eight to twelve feet along one wall, about five or six feet deep. Hides or blankets hung from a crosspiece to divide the area for privacy. These houses were very smoky, especially in bad weather when smoke holes had to be covered. But the smoke helped to keep out insects. In good weather, most cooking was done outside. Corn was pounded with a pestle in a mortar to make cornmeal and food prepared for winter.

Since most travel was by water, usually by canoe, villages were often located near a river or lake. In the more northern areas, canoes were made by covering a lightweight framework with birchbark. The Iroquois made similar, but heavier, canoes of elm bark. Canoes were made waterproof by covering joints with pitch (tar).

Other tribes used dugout canoes. To make a dugout, the men burned the

One Family's space at end of a long house, is shown here. The child is talking to a baby in a cradleboard. His mother brings a basket of berries. Outside the fire rack can be seen.

Storage shelf

Bow and quiver

Seating and sleeping shelf

base of a good-sized tree to fell it. Then a fire was made on one side of the log and carefully controlled. The charred wood was scraped away until the proper shape was achieved. Most dugouts held one or two persons, but early explorers told of large sea-going canoes that carried eight or ten warriors and possibly were used for deep-sea fishing.

To Complete Diorama

MATERIALS: (depending on what you make): natural sticks and twigs (from fallen branches), papier maché (Celluclay—mix as directed), or modeling clay (preferably self-hardening); balsa wood, yellow wax, glue, thread, and needle; string or cord; scraps of fake fur, fabric, felt, or chamois; brown paint; cornhusks; lightweight card; sandpaper; awl; knife to whittle shapes.

To establish the proper scale for these units, determine how tall a person would be in the house you constructed;

about 1/3 the height of a longhouse, 1/2 the height of a wigwam (Fig. 1). Draw "person height" on paper as a guide.

Make pots, boxes and bowls of balsa wood, papier maché or clay. Cover door with felt or chamois shaped to look like an animal skin. Make cooking fires of twigs glued to card (Fig. 2). Roll scraps of fabric, tie and place on storage shelves. Make a bark box of heavy paper covered with brown crepe paper (Fig. 3). Fold in ends and glue (Fig. 4).

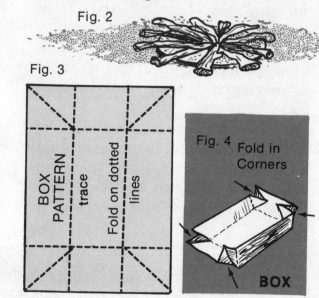

Fig. 2

Fig. 3

BOX PATTERN trace Fold on dotted lines

Fig. 4 Fold in Corners

BOX

Fig. 1

For scale in diorama determine "Person Height"

Iroquois cooking pot

Wooden bowls

Ladle   Box   Troughs   Mortar   Pestle

20

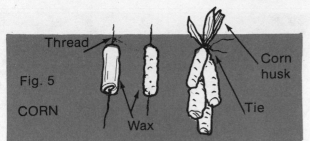

Fig. 5

CORN

Thread

Corn husk

Wax

Tie

Person Height

Fig. 7

LEATHER STRETCHING

For dried corn, take small piece of yellow candle wax or wax from around cheese. Roll it around piece of thread (Fig. 5). With thread, tie in some narrow strips of corn husks at the top. Tie on posts.

Make a hanging rack of forked twigs over outside fire (Fig. 6). See height in Fig. 1. Add glue and insert ends into base. Hang pot or box from crosspiece. Lay twigs nearby for supply of firewood.

chamois or felt to fit the rack (Fig. 7). Wet chamois and sew to rack.

For storage bags (Chippewa), cut tan fabric (Fig.8). Glue edges and tie to post or place on shelf (Fig. 9). Make a bag-weaving rack similar to drying rack (Fig. 10).

Fig. 6

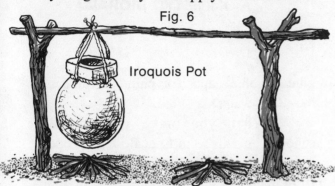

Iroquois Pot

Hanging racks

Fig. 8

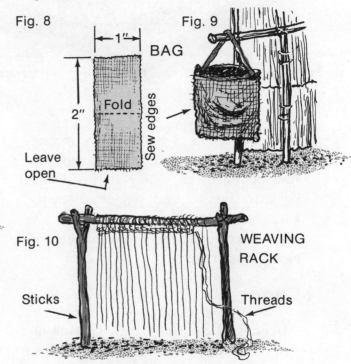

1"

BAG

2"

Fold

Sew edges

Leave open

Fig. 9

Chippewa Pot

Fig. 10

WEAVING RACK

Sticks

Threads

For leather drying rack, cut two vertical sticks person height, add glue, and insert ends in the ground. Lash and glue on two horizontal sticks. Cut a piece of

Find a dried branch that looks like a tree, make a hole in the base, and glue in position to complete diorama (Fig. 11). If you have a small plastic dog the right size, put him in the scene. The Indians had many dogs around their homes.

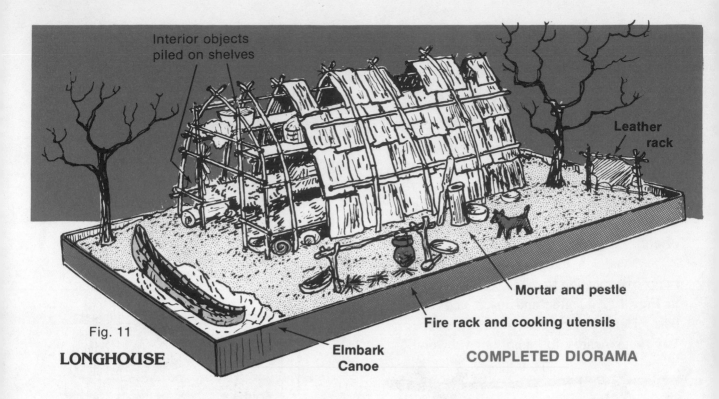

Interior objects
piled on shelves

Leather
rack

Mortar and pestle

Fire rack and cooking utensils

Fig. 11

LONGHOUSE

Elmbark
Canoe

COMPLETED DIORAMA

Accessories and house coverings can determine the area your diorama represents. Most areas used pottery as well as baskets, boxes, and wooden utensils. Birchbark was used in northern areas only. Shells were used for dishes and utensils along coastal areas.

Canoes

MATERIALS: Blue paper (or paint and brush), top of maché egg carton or produce tray from supermarket, crepe paper, reed, glue, black marker, clip clothespins, needle and heavy thread. For dugout: balsa wood, masking tape, sandpaper, knife, brown paint and brush.

Along one edge of the diorama, glue on blue paper (or paint the area to look like water).

When you make your model canoe, you will want to scale it to proper proportion. Canoe size was anywhere from 16 to 30 feet or about three or four times as long as your person-guide. Cut edges from maché tray to get a flat piece of card. Decide length to fit onto this cut piece. Make proper canoe for type of house.

BIRCHBARK CANOE:

Draw a line on paper. Draw one side of canoe (Fig. 1), with curved ends for Great Lakes area, or straighter ends for a New England canoe (Fig. 2). Fold on line; trace other side. Open and trace on

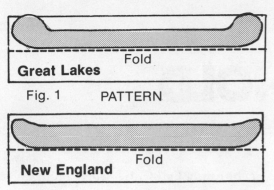

Fold

Great Lakes

Fig. 1   PATTERN

Fold

New England

Fig. 2

card. Cut out. Cover both sides with tan crepe paper, wrinkling it to look like birchbark.

For ribs, measure (Fig. 3) and cut three pieces of reed slightly less than width of card. Wet reed and bend to U shape. While canoe is still damp from paste, curve around and glue ends together. Hold with clip clothespins. Add glue to ribs (reeds) and glue in place, holding with clips. When dry, cut two pieces of reed, each the length of the top edge. Glue and sew on (Fig. 4). Sew ends also.

Fig. 3

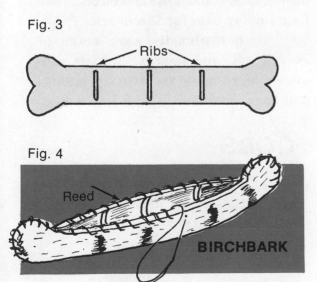

Ribs

Fig. 4

Reed

BIRCHBARK

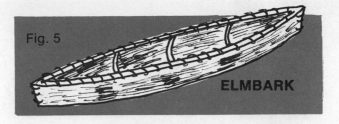

Fig. 5

ELMBARK

ELM BARK CANOE:

Make the same with straight ends. Cover with dark brown crepe paper. Add ribs and top reeds (Fig. 5) and sew on. Use marker to dab with black to look like the pitch.

DUGOUT:

To make a dugout-type canoe, shape two ends out of balsa wood (Fig. 6). Cut maché card piece as long as possible and wide enough to fit around the shaped ends (Fig. 7). Wet piece, add glue to balsa ends, and shape maché card around them. Hold with tape. When glue is dry, taper edges (Fig. 8) into the wood. Paint dark brown. Entire canoe can be whittled of balsa instead. Sand smooth and paint.

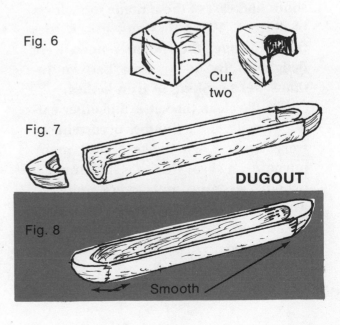

Fig. 6

Cut two

Fig. 7

DUGOUT

Fig. 8

Smooth

2 HOUSEHOLD

Did you ever hear of stone boiling? It's a method of cooking. A hot stone was lifted out of the fire with sticks, then dropped into a wood or bark vessel containing stew or other liquid. The hot rock heated the liquid. When the rock cooled, another hot rock was dropped in. This continued until the food was cooked.

The Indians used wood, bark or clay pots to cook in, as they had no metal pots. However, clay pots were clumsy and breakable, and tribes that moved about usually used wooden containers. The Iroquois and most tribes south and east of them made some form of pottery. When they saw iron kettles from Europe, the Indian women were delighted. By 1640, most Eastern Indians were cooking in iron kettles.

To clean the kettle and other eating utensils, small bundles of corn husks were used. Corn husks served many purposes; a sheaf tied to a stick made a broom, sleeping mats were made of woven husks. For a thick doormat, corn husks were braided with tufts of protruding ends. Husks were braided into ropes or hammocks. Cobs were good scrubbers.

After the meat was removed from deer, other parts served many uses. Hides were made into leather for clothing, curtains, coverings, and storage bags. Antlers and bones could be shaped into tools, handles, needles, and utensils. The sinew was their sewing thread and bowstrings. Tail hairs, dyed, made embroidery thread, tassels, and the roach headdress.

The Indians knew what kind of tree provided the best wood for a particular need. They used bark, inner bark (withes), and wood to carve dishes, ladles, troughs, and boxes. They found many uses for birchbark.

Other utensils were made of horn, shell, and gourds. Storage containers were made by weaving baskets and bags, and sewing bark into boxes.

FOODS

For food the Indians hunted game, deer, small animals and wild birds: duck, turkey and wild pigeons.

They fished with lines and nets.

Many tribes also farmed, growing corn, squash, and beans primarily. Corn was pounded to make flour and prepared in many ways. Wild foods such as berries, roots, and nuts were gathered. Wild onion and garlic were added to nut oils to flavor meats. Sassafras, witch hazel, and other herbs and roots were gathered for medicinal purposes.

In the spring, they would tap the trees in northern areas to get the "sweet water," maple syrup. This was their only flavoring and was used in many foods. One early French explorer returned home to tell of a delicacy served him by Indians made of two ingredients not known to Europeans at the time: popcorn covered with maple syrup.

The Indians cooked the main meal in the morning; everyone ate by midmorning. Food was left simmering over the fire with corn cakes and other food nearby, for anyone who felt hungry during the day.

Recipes

SWEETENED SQUASH:

Acorn squash, corn oil, maple syrup, nuts.

Vary amounts to suit your taste and the size of the squash. Bake squash about one hour; let cool slightly. Cut squash in half, being careful of escaping steam. (You may need some help with this). Scoop out seeds and discard. Scoop squash from its shell into a dish. Add two tablespoons of corn oil or butter, about two tablespoons of maple syrup, and some chopped walnuts. Mix well and replace in shell. Put into oven just long enough to heat thoroughly and blend the flavors. Serve in the squash shells.

ROASTED CORN:

Use a campfire or outdoor grill. Select ears with a good layer of husks still in place. To saturate husks, soak in a pan of water. With tongs, place wet ears along the edge of the fire in hot ashes, near the hot coals. Turn occasionally. Corn should be done in about one-half hour or less, depending on how hot the coals are.

WEAVING

The Indians were adept at weaving and made many kinds of mats and bags for their homes using cedar bark, corn husks, basswood fibers, cattail reeds, rushes, or sweetgrass. Reeds and cattails not supple enough to weave were held together by piercing. Basswood fibers were pushed through wet reeds to make mats, or fibers were twined around to hold the reeds together. Mats had many uses: large ones

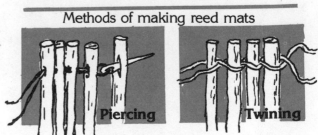

Methods of making reed mats

Piercing   Twining

25

to cover the house, softer ones for beds, sturdy ones for the floor. In winter extra mats were hung on the inside walls for warmth.

For bags they devised a method by which both sides and bottom were woven at the same time with no seams. In the Great Lakes region, the twined method was used for large storage bags for household goods, as large as 18″ or 20″ wide. Smaller twined bags held sacred objects (charms) and had more elaborate, woven designs of special significance. Bags for general use had simple geometric designs. Dyed moose or elk hair was used for color in designs. By the nineteenth century, cotton and wool yarn, obtained in trade, was used.

The Ojibway loom was a stick supported horizontally. Cords hung on it were left loose at the bottom ends. One could weave around both sides and create a bag with no side seams. You can make a sturdy twined bag of this type using an old picture frame for a loom.

Twined Bag

MATERIALS: Old picture frame (about 8″ x 10″), two or three colors of cord or yarn (macramé cords, wrapping twine, heavy string), two tacks.

Select a combination of cords, all about the same thickness, such as brown twine, white string, and a bright-colored yarn. For the verticals, use a firm, smooth cord such as twine.

To start, cut a piece of twine, wrap the frame twice, and tie tightly. Place a tack at each side to hold in place (Fig. 1). The frame is the width of the bag. Decide what length you wish the bag to be. For a 9″ bag, plus 4″ of fringe, add an extra inch to get 14″ length. Double this measurement (28″). Cut about 30 cords this length

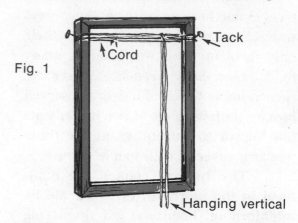

Fig. 1

Cord

Tack

Hanging vertical

for hanging verticals. Attach to the twine on the frame, knotting as shown (Fig. 2). Go around, covering horizontal twine front and back. Hanging cords should be about 1/4″ apart.

For twining, cut a piece of cord about four feet long. Fold in half and twist around a hanging cord at one side. Hold both pair of twining cords in one hand,

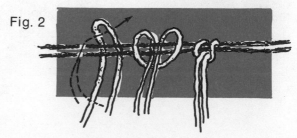

Fig. 2

manipulate hanging cords with the other hand. Make a twist with the twining cords, pull one hanging cord between, make another twist, and continue (Fig. 3).

Fig. 3

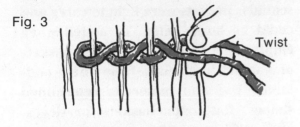
Twist

This is the basic stitch (Fig. 4). Go around and around, row after row. Push up to the top, pushing each new row against the previous row. When twining cords run out, tie on new ones. After the bag is finished, the ends of ties can be pulled inside and clipped.

Fig. 4

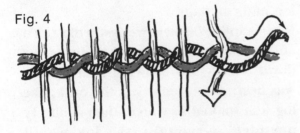

Try two different colors for a pair of twining cords. It will make a pattern in the weaving. For change of texture or design, reverse the twist. If you have been making an up-over twist, try a down-under twist (Fig. 5).

Fig. 5

For stripes, use both pair of cords the same color for several rows, then change the color of both cords when you tie on new ones.

When the bag is woven, do not cut twining cords. Remove tacks and slip the bag off the frame. Hold front and back together at bottom edge. To close the bottom, twine across, taking a front and back cord between each twist each time. Go across twice and tie twining cords at edge. Now tie each pair of hanging cords around the twining cords (Fig. 6) to hold twining

Fig. 6   Tie

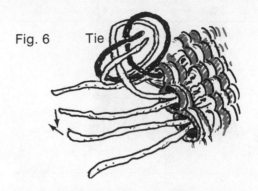

cords securely and make a firm bottom on the bag (Fig. 7).

Hanging cords make a fringe. Tie on extra cords if you'd like a thicker fringe. Trim even.

Fig. 7

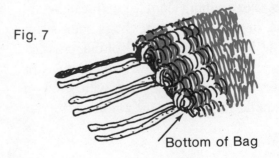
Bottom of Bag

For handle, tie on a piece of heavy cord (Fig. 8) or a leather thong. Or the handle can be braided or woven. Hang on a hook to store your special possessions.

Fig. 8

ALTERNATES: Beads can be added to verticals while weaving is in progress, or tied into the fringe for added interest.

The twining method can make a sturdy bag from difficult or odd materials. For instance, use plastic twine for verticals. For twining cords, cut bread wrappers or colored plastic bags into strips about 1 1/2″ wide. Twine, folding or twisting strips as you work, making strips about 1/4″ wide. Alternate with rows of synthetic raffia for solid colors.

BASKETS

Every household needed containers to carry, gather, and store essentials. Baskets were light to carry and could be hung, piled, or nested when empty. The Indians made fine baskets of various materials from the woodlands. Use and materials determined shapes: flat, open baskets for sieves, corn washing or berry drying; deep, tight baskets to store corn, flour or other foods. Light baskets were good for berry and nut gathering. Reed baskets were made of willow shoots. Corn husks or bundles of sweet grass or other fibers were twined with cord to make baskets, using methods similar to making mats or bags.

Splint baskets were sturdiest. To obtain the splints, a small tree was cut down. Black ash growing in a swamp was best. After removing the bark, the log was soaked in water, then skillfully pounded. Gradually the log would separate and split along the annual growth rings. The outside layer of splints would be pulled off and pounding continued. Rings in a good growth year might be as heavy as one-fourth inch thick. These were saved for handles or other uses. The thinner rings

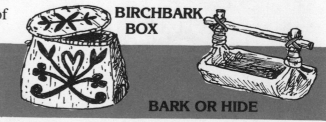

BIRCHBARK BOX

BARK OR HIDE

were better for basket weaving. Splints were cut into widths needed; a variety of widths made interesting patterns when woven. Usually, the natural color variations of brown and tans made attractive baskets, but sometimes splints were dyed. Using the wood splints wet, a basket was woven.

Some tribes decorated their baskets with stamped-on designs. A piece of soft wood or the cut side of a potato was carved to form a design. Or a decoration could be created with the end of a rolled piece of rawhide or a bundle of sticks tied together. The Micmac and Onandaga made especially attractive splint baskets.

STAMPS

rolled hide

sticks

Splint Type Basket

MATERIALS: Brown wrapping paper, wallpaper paste, glue, clip clothespins or stationery clips, wax paper, newspapers, masking tape, push pins, lightweight card, scrap of wood, hammer. Optional: potato, paring knife, stamp pad (or paint).

Plan size of basket you wish to make to determine the length of the splints. Figure the width of the base, plus twice the height (Fig. 1), and add at least 5″, to get the length of the vertical splints.

Measure to determine length of vertical splints

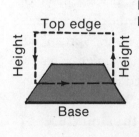

Top edge

Height

Base

Height

For instance:

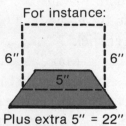

6″   6″

5″

Plus extra 5″ = 22″ long splints

Fig. 1

To determine length of horizontal splints (weavers)

Add four sides plus 3″ = 23″

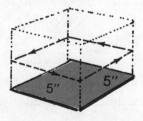

5″   5″

For horizontals (weavers), figure the distance needed to go around the base, then add 3″. For instance, to make a basket 6″ high and 5″ square: for verticals, add 5″ (base) + 12″ (twice height) + 5″ extra = 22″. For weavers, add 5″ + 5″ + 5″ + 5″ (the four sides of the base) + 3″ extra = 23″. Be generous. You can always cut off anything left over.

To make splints, cut brown wrapping paper various widths (4½″ to 7″) to length needed (22″ to 23″). A 4½″-wide strip makes about a ½″-wide splint; a 7″-wide strip makes about a 1″-wide splint. Make three or four different widths.

Lay newspaper on a large flat surface (or floor). Over this, place a piece of waxed paper longer than the distance end-to-end of your longest strip. Spread out more newspapers and have plenty handy so fresh ones can be used as the first ones get sticky.

Make a very thin mixture of wallpaper paste. Take a strip of brown paper, lay on newspapers, and spread with paste. With hands still wet with paste, fold strip lengthwise approximately in thirds (Fig. 2, A & B). Crease and fold the folded piece again, this time overlapping sides to center (Fig 2, C & D). Add paste along overlap. Strip should be saturated with paste. Wipe off excess. Lay over onto waxed paper to dry. Press down occasionally to flatten and make sure paste holds.

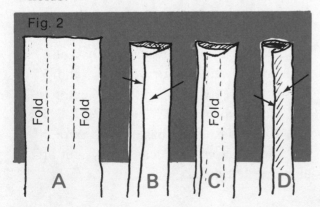

Fig. 2
Fold Fold Fold
A B C D

Make all your own strips or use some commercially made strips. H.H. Perkins (see suppliers), carries paper fiber ½″-wide splints. Number of splints needed will depend on basket size and width of strips. Prepare about 15 strips, ¾″ to 1¼″ wide. About a dozen ½″ strips will probably be needed also.

To start weaving, lay one strip across another (Fig. 3). Place on a scrap of wood and add push pins to help maintain

Fig. 3

right angles of starting pieces (or use masking tape to hold position). Add one strip each side, weaving strips through

Fig. 4
Add Add
Weave in
Weave in

(Fig. 4), across strips already placed. Continue weaving over and under (Fig. 5), alternating wide and narrow strips. Push strips together as closely as possible.

When planned base area is woven (5″ square, for instance), cut a piece of card this size. Remove original pins. Place

Fig. 5

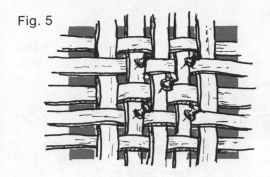

card over woven base (Fig. 6), and pin down. Hammer the push pins into the board if necessary. The card helps to establish and maintain the square base.

Fig. 6

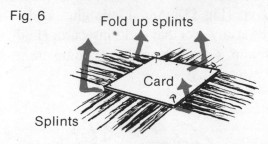

Fold up splints

Card

Splints

Fold up all splints along edge of card. Take a weaver strip and place behind one vertical splint, starting at middle of one side (see Fig. 8). Hold with clip clothespin. Weave over and under, going around basket, making sure each over or under is opposite base weaving (Fig. 7).

Fig. 7

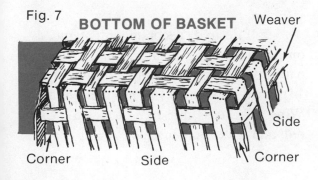

BOTTOM OF BASKET

Weaver

Corner   Side   Side   Corner

Bend weaver splint as you come to each corner. Hold with clip if splints tend to slip. First two rows are hardest. End behind vertical (Fig. 8) overlap.

Fig. 8

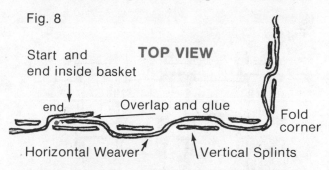

TOP VIEW

Start and end inside basket

end   Overlap and glue   Fold corner

Horizontal Weaver   Vertical Splints

Cut next weaver strip, start in the middle on a different side from the first one. Clip in place (Fig. 9) and weave

Fig. 9

Fold Corner   New Weaver

around. Overlap ends when you get back to the start of strip (Fig. 8). Hold with clip until next row is completed.

Crease weaver at each corner for three rows. Upper rows do not need creasing. This makes a basket square on the bottom, round at the top. After three or four rows, the basket may be removed from the board, as its shape will be formed. Continue weaving, using various width strips (Fig. 10) to give an interesting look to the weave. Start on different sides each row.

Fig. 10

For the last two rows, use 1/2" weaver strips. There should be at least 2" of verticals above the last row. After completing, cut another 1/2"-wide strip.

To finish the top lay the extra strip outside, parallel with last strip (Fig. 11). Fold a vertical splint down over extra

Fig. 11

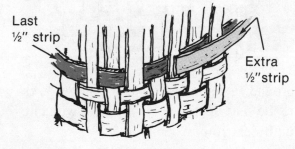

Last 1/2" strip

Extra 1/2" strip

strip. Determine length needed. Trim vertical and insert behind a weaver (Fig. 12). Fold down next splint and repeat. Lengths will alternate as needed to go behind

Fig. 12

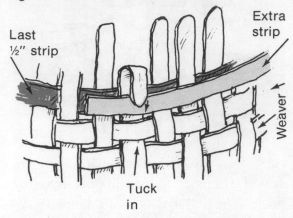

Last 1/2" strip

Extra strip

Weaver

Tuck in

weavers (Fig. 13). Add a little glue, if desired, at any spot that looks insecure. Hold with clip. Continue around to complete.

Fig. 13

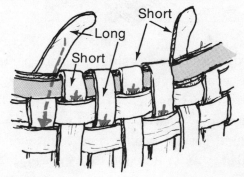

Long

Short

Short

If desired, decorate with stamped-on designs. Cut a potato in half. With a paring knife, make a simple design (Fig. 14) small enough to fit on wider splints. Wipe off excess moisture on potato. Use red and black commercial stamp pads.

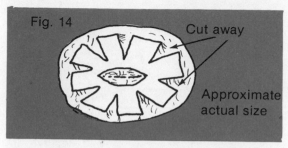

Fig. 14

Cut away

Approximate actual size

Press design on red pad, then onto basket (Fig. 15) in several places. Make another design on the other half potato, and press on black pad and onto other splints. Or put a thin layer of paint on the design, then stamp on splints before paint dries.

Fig. 15

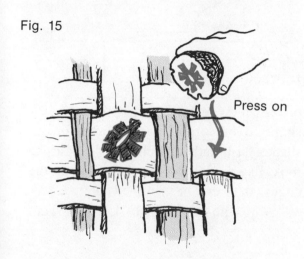

Press on

ALTERNATES: Try using various light and dark or colored papers to make splints. You can make a big waste basket, as these paper splint baskets are remarkably sturdy. For a conversation piece, make a basket of newspaper splints: the comics or sport pages or want ads . . .

BIRCHBARK

The white birch trees in the northern areas of the woodlands were utilized in many ways by the Indians of those areas. Birchbark was waterproof and resisted decay. Larger pieces were used for house coverings and canoes. A small rolled piece, when lit on the end, became a light. Night fishing and hunting were often done by the light of a birch torch.

A tree cut in the spring had a thick, brown layer under the white outer layer of bark. Summer bark was thinner with little of the brown layer. Boxes, baskets, cups, trays, funnels, fans, and other utensils were shaped and sewn, usually with the white layer inside.

For decorations, containers were embroidered with spruce roots, moose hair, or porcupine quills. Brown and white designs, usually florals or animals, were created by scraping away parts of the outer layer of the box. If the

Cone (For Maple sugar)

Fan

Box

Spoon

box was made of summer bark, designs might be cut out and sewn on.

Some containers were simple pieces of folded birchbark. Some had handles. Shape, size and construction varied according to use, from small ones for gathering berries to huge storage boxes holding twelve quarts or more.

With pitch on the seams, birchbark containers were waterproof and could be used to carry water, collect maple syrup or for cooking. A birchbark vessel full of liquid could be hung over a fire and would not burn, as long as the fire was not higher than the level of the liquid inside.

Bark Box (Mocuck)

MATERIALS: Brown or orange oaktag, brown and tan crepe paper, tan paper, plain paper, wallpaper paste, buttonhole thread and needle, glue.

On a piece of paper, draw shape of dimensions shown (Fig. 1). This is ¼ of the pattern. On the oaktag, draw an area 12″ × 20″. Mark center lines and draw shape in each quarter (Fig. 2). Cut out. Also cut a strip ½″ wide by 20″ long. Draw decoration shown (Fig. 3); draw other half, trace onto tan paper, and cut out.

Mix wallpaper paste. Cut a piece

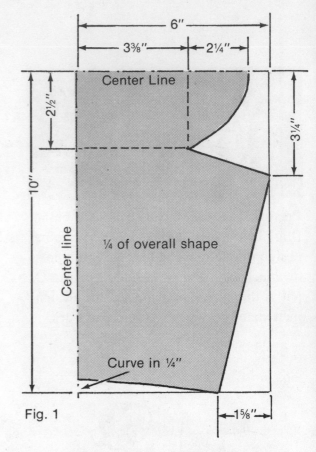

Fig. 1

of brown crepe paper larger than the box shape. Glue crepe paper onto cut-out shape. Push and scrunch into wrinkles to look like bark. Don't worry about the edges; they can be trimmed later. Cover ½″ strip with brown also. Let dry. Turn

Fig. 2

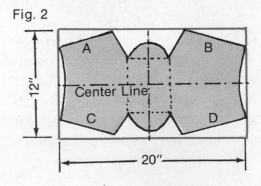

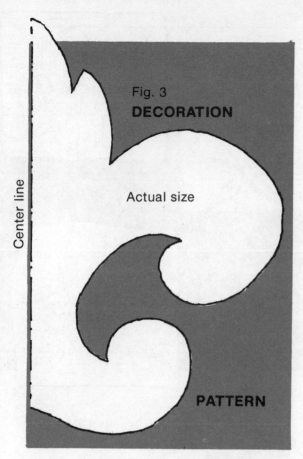

Fig. 3
DECORATION

Center line

Actual size

PATTERN

over and cover other side with brown, creating texture as before. Cover paper cut-out decoration (Fig. 3) with white crepe paper. Let dry.

Trim edges even. Fold box shape (see dotted lines in Fig. 1). Thread needle and knot end. Bring sides A/B together (Fig.4), overlap about ½″ and sew. Repeat, sewing sides C/D together. Fold up

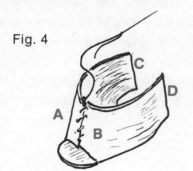

Fig. 4

base ends and sew to sides. To finish top, lay the ½″ strip around the outside and sew (Fig. 5), going over top and coming back out from inside.

Trim edges even on white decoration. Glue to side of box (Fig. 6).

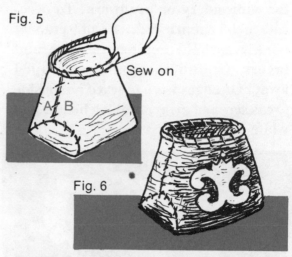

Fig. 5

Sew on

Fig. 6

ALTERNATE: Instead of glued-on decoration, a design or animal or flower shape could be painted on with white paint (Fig. 7).

The top edge could be a reed or splint, if preferred.

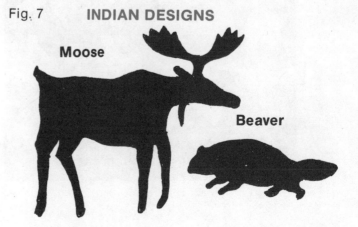

Fig. 7   **INDIAN DESIGNS**

Moose

Beaver

BITTEN BARK TRANSPARENCIES

Small scraps of birchbark were cut into shapes for stencils or patterns for embroidery or beadwork. To decorate a birchbark box, a cut scrap of bark was held against the box and layers around the pattern scraped away. Or edges were marked and inside areas scraped away, making brown and white decorations.

TRANSPARENCIES

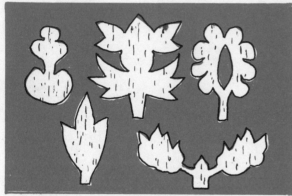

Cutout Birchbark Pattern Shapes

Cutout shapes that may have been used as toys for children

Birchbark can be separated into layers, some paper-thin. Possibly as amusement or to create new design ideas, young Chippewa women made "gnawed" bark pieces. A thin scrap was heated slightly to make it more flexible, then folded. With her sharp eyeteeth and a slight grinding motion, she would bite through all the folded layers. When bark was unfolded, light would shine through the holes, forming a lacy decoration. The small, slitlike holes in the bark might have been used for a guide for beadwork designs.

Our eyeteeth today have not been worn as sharp as an Indian's, but it is fun to make punched-hole-type designs.

Hole Designs

MATERIALS: Thin paper (lightweight typing, onion skin or similar paper), small paring knife, scrap piece of wood, masking tape. Optional: screwdriver, colored paper, paste.

Fold paper as shown (Fig. 1). Lay folded paper on the scrap of wood. For a tool, wrap a piece of paper around edge of paring knife and tape around several times, leaving only the tip exposed.

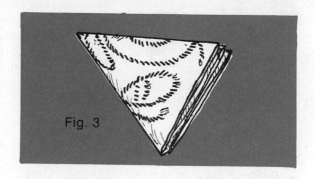

Fig. 3

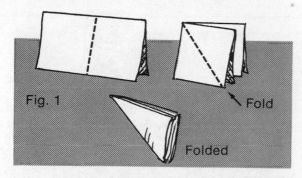

Fig. 1

Fold

Folded

Push the tip of the knife down into folded paper, making rows of holes through all layers (Fig. 2). Make curved designs and rows of holes (Fig. 3). Create

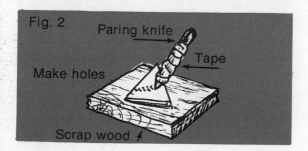

Fig. 2

Paring knife

Tape

Make holes

Scrap wood

your own designs. Try other tools to vary shapes of holes. Larger holes can be made by pushing tip of screwdriver through paper layers. Create your design as you go along. (The Indian women did not see what they were biting.) Try various folds.

After holes are made, open paper to see design. Refold and make more holes in places where needed. Unfold and hang in the window so light will shine through the holes (Fig. 4). Or make the outside row of holes fairly close together. Tear along edges and mount design on colored paper (Fig. 5).

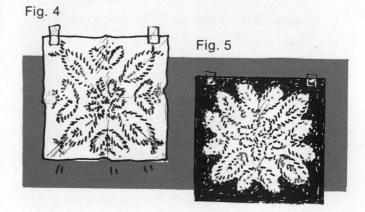

Fig. 4

Fig. 5

3 CLOTHING

The Indians of the Northeast had to cope with extremes of climate—long, bitter winters and hot summers that brought multitudes of biting insects. Protective clothing was a necessity.

Most garments were made of deerskin. The stiff hide was processed into a soft, pliable leather, and smoked to give it color and suppleness. Shapes were cut with sharp stone tools and sewed with bone needles, using sinew or vegetable fibers. As the process was tedious, there was little shaping or sewing.

The men and boys wore a breechclout, a strip of leather worn between the legs and folded over a belt front and back. For ceremonial occasions, an apron or kilt was worn over the breechclout. Leggings were a necessity in many areas—in winter for warmth, in summer for protection against woodland brambles and insect bites. Early explorers of the Lower Hudson Valley told of fabulous cloaks made of turkey feathers worn by the Indians of that area. Occasionally shirts were worn, usually for ceremonial pur-

poses. Decorative sashes with long fringes were tied across the shoulder or wound around the waist where they could hold a bag or axe. There were no pockets. The Indians used natural fibers to weave sashes and garters, but did not weave clothing fabric.

Eastern Indian (as depicted by early European settlers).

The women wore a long skirt tied about the waist or up under the arms, usually a wrap style, leaving one thigh exposed for rolling fibers. Women's leggings were knee-high. In cold weather, they wore a sort of poncho or capelike top over the shoulders and blankets.

For severe weather, blankets of hide, with the fur left on, served everyone both for sleeping and for wearing outside in the cold. Narrow strips of rabbit fur were woven into a warp of fibers. The result was a thick, warm blanket with fur on both sides. The children wore little clothing. In winter they wrapped up in the fur blankets.

To cover and protect their feet, the Indians wore moccasins (an Algonquian word). Most woodland styles had a center seam over the toes, some with a small insert. There was no right or left

and they were rotated for longer wear. Moccasins were decorated, as the Indians believed attractive footwear was important to show respect for the land the feet must tread upon. For walking in swamps or during bitter winters, a covering was made of heavier leather (usually bear, moose, or muskrat), and dried moss was stuffed inside to add extra warmth. The Iroquois often wore corn husk sandals in summer.

Clothing styles and decorations varied among the tribes. Everyday clothing usually had little ornamentation, but for ceremonial purposes garments were decorated as attractively as possible to show gratitude to "the giver of all things." Dyed moose hair, porcupine quills, shell beads, bones and seeds were sewn on. Dewclaws, the cone-shaped tip of a deer hoof, produced a rattling sound when sewn along a garment edge.

With the arrival of Europeans, the Indians were quick to appreciate the value of woven cloth, for which they traded as early as 1540. As their furs were much in demand by Europeans, the Indians could obtain, in exchange, not only cloth but beads, silk ribbons and yarns for decoration, and thread, and metal needles. Clothing became easier to sew and decorate. When metals became available, the Indians made cones of tin to replace dewclaws, and worked jewelry of silver and other metals.

MOCCASINS

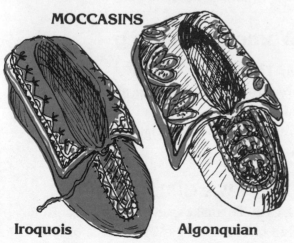

Iroquois   **Algonquian**

Center puckered seam covered with bead or quillwork

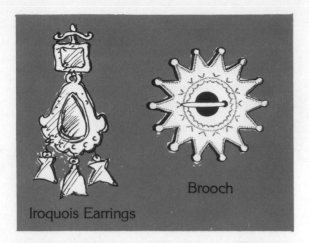

Iroquois Earrings

Brooch

Although most tribes continued to use durable deerskin for everyday clothing, they made more elegant garments for special occasions, usually with dark blue, black, or red wool or velvet decorated with exquisite beadwork. Designs were sometimes geometric, but were usually florals as tribute to the natural beauty around them. Ceremonial garments included beaded vests, large decorative bags, capes, aprons, garters, and sashes. Spectators as well as participants in the ceremonies felt obliged to wear the finest clothes they could make.

Some tribes adapted European styles of the seventeenth and eighteenth centuries. Others adapted their own styles to fabrics. An Iroquois woman might have added a calico dress over a leather skirt and leggings with beaded edges. By the nineteenth century most tribes along the eastern coast had absorbed the styles of the colonists.

CLOTHING BEFORE EUROPEAN INFLUENCES

Doll-Size Models

MATERIALS:—General (for most all doll clothing): Fabric, scraps of bright-colored yarn, tissue paper (for patterns), needle and thread, glue, felt markers (two or three colors), decorative tapes (1/4″ wide or less), or seed beads.

To look like buckskin, fabric should be tan-colored felt, cotton, or suede cloth. Or use old sheet, dyed tan. Most fabrics can be ravelled to make fringes. Leftover scraps of chamois can be glued to the edge of the fabric and cut into a fringe. For making doll clothes, chamois looks the most like Indian leather, but it can be expensive. Seams can be glued, but sewing on the fabric is best.

Women's Clothing

MATERIALS: See above, plus adult-proportioned female doll about 8″ to 10″ tall (or any size). Choose a doll preferably with dark hair and straight feet (not angled for heels).

CHIPPEWA GIRL:
Dress: To make pattern, measure from chin to below knees. Cut a piece of tissue

paper this length. Fold top over 1/2" and wrap around the doll, overlapping about 3/4". Mark width and cut.

Legging: To make pattern, measure from mid-thigh to ankle. Cut a paper strip this width, wrap around the leg loosely, and mark. Add 1/4" for seam each side. Using paper patterns, cut two leggings and a dress out of the fabric. Sew up the legging seam and turn right side out. Place on leg, with the bottom just below the ankle. Tie just above the knee (Fig. 1). Fold down. Cut a piece of yarn and tie below the knee, allowing ends to hang. Ravel edge or cut fringe. Repeat on other leg.

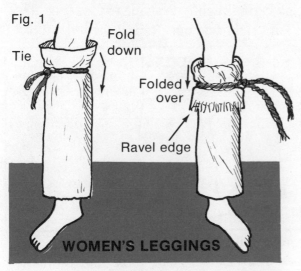

Fig. 1
Tie
Fold down
Folded over
Ravel edge

WOMEN'S LEGGINGS

Wrap dress around and overlap on the side (Fig. 2). Tie under armpits and fold top down 1/2". For strap, cut strip about 1/4" wide, long enough to go over shoulder. Glue or sew in place, tucking behind dress top, front, and back (Fig. 3).

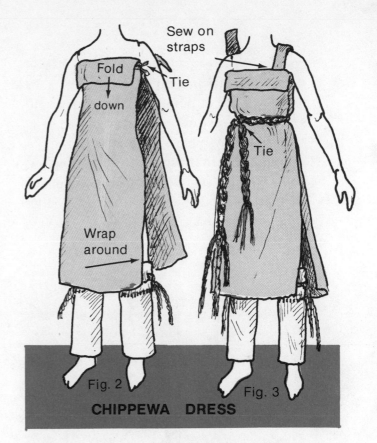

Sew on straps
Fold down
Tie
Wrap around
Tie
Fig. 2
Fig. 3

CHIPPEWA DRESS

Repeat on other shoulder. Braid some colorful yarn and tie at waist. Ends can hang to ankles.

Sleeves: For separate sleeves, measure wrist circumference and add 1/8". Draw on paper. Measure from wrist to center neck at back (length A in Fig. 4). Side B is the same length as A. Length C is from neck to waist plus 1/2". Draw on paper,

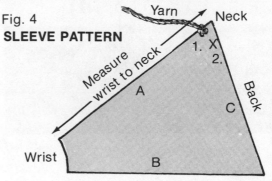

Fig. 4
SLEEVE PATTERN
Yarn
Neck
Measure wrist to neck
1. X 2.
A
Back
C
Wrist
B

make pattern, cut two of fabric. Sew a 3″ piece of yarn at point 1 (Side A) on each sleeve. Wrap sleeve around wrist and sew together. Sew other sleeve at wrist.

Tie yarn (from points 1) in front on doll (Fig. 5), and sew together at center back at points 2 (Side C). Ends of C side hang loose in back (Fig. 6).

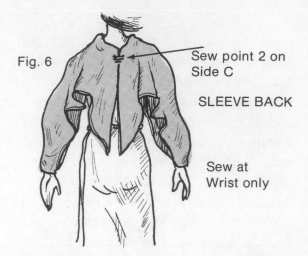

Fig. 6

Sew point 2 on Side C

SLEEVE BACK

Sew at Wrist only

Fig. 5

Tie

Sew

Sew

CHIPPEWA GIRL

Moccasins: For pattern, place feet on paper (Fig. 7) and trace around. Draw shape shown; cut two of felt or fabric. Fold in half, wrong side out, and sew toe, gathering slightly to shape to foot (Fig. 8). Turn right side out. Repeat for other foot.

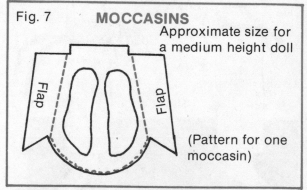

Fig. 7

MOCCASINS

Approximate size for a medium height doll

Flap

Flap

(Pattern for one moccasin)

With felt marker, make tiny dots of color on flaps (Fig. 9) to look like quill or beadwork. Sew beads along toe pucker if desired. Place on doll (Fig. 10), fitting onto foot. Trim off any excess at back and sew up each back seam. Wrap a piece of string around ankle under flap (Fig. 11), and tie in back.

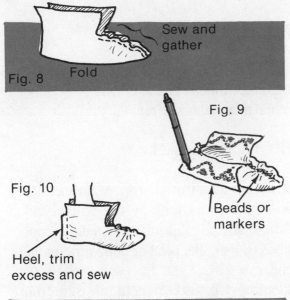

Fig. 8   Sew and gather   Fold

Fig. 9

Fig. 10   Beads or markers

Heel, trim excess and sew

Fig. 11   Tie in Back

Hair: If possible, make a single braid in back. Tie with yarns or decorative strips, wrapping around the braid. Leave long ends hanging (Fig. 12).

Fig. 12

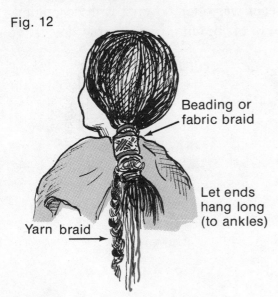

Beading or fabric braid

Yarn braid

Let ends hang long (to ankles)

IROQUOIS GIRL:

Leggings and moccasins are similar. For skirt, measure from waist to ankle, cut paper, and wrap around to determine width. Cut out fabric and wrap around waist, overlapping at right. Tie and fold down about 1/4″ (Fig. 13). Bottom edge can be fringed.

To make the cape that Iroquois women wore in cold weather, lay your doll, with arms slightly spread, on paper and draw around shoulders. Mark X at each armpit. Add 1/8″ for seam (Fig. 14).

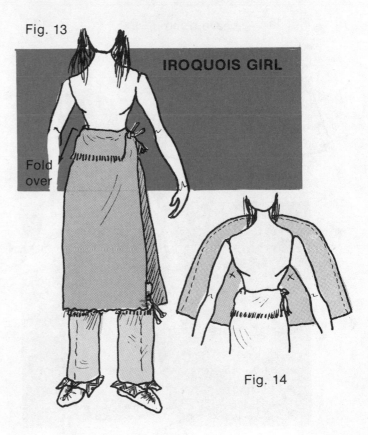

Fig. 13   IROQUOIS GIRL

Fold over

Fig. 14

Measure from shoulder to just below waist and draw on pattern. Cut two of tissue paper and try on the doll. Adjust, if needed, and cut out of fabric. Glue or sew side seams, leaving them open at center top to get the doll's head through. Turn right side out and try on. Cut two arm slits in front (Fig. 15). Remove and color on a decoration with markers. Fringe bottom edge if possible. Place on doll. Sew front to back at X on pattern. Hair was worn in one or two braids with little decoration (Fig. 16).

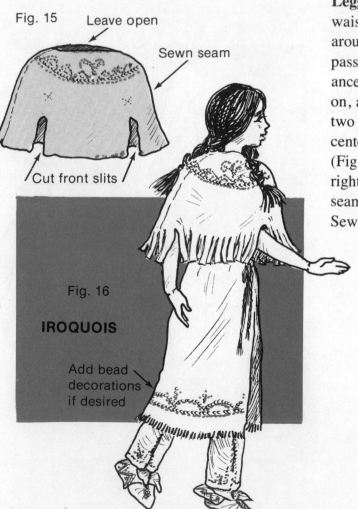

Fig. 15
Leave open
Sewn seam
Cut front slits

Fig. 16

IROQUOIS

Add bead decorations if desired

Male Clothing

MATERIALS: Male doll about 8″ to 10″. Increase dimensions if doll is larger. For other materials, see previous project.

IROQUOIS MAN:

Breechclout: Cut a strip of fabric 3/4″ wide, about as long as the doll is tall. Fringe edges. With markers, add decorations to look like bead or quillwork on one end.

Leggings: To make pattern, measure from waist to ankle. Measure circumference around leg, just large enough so foot can pass through. Add 1/4″ for seam allowance. Cut a rectangle of paper this size, try on, and pin in place. Adjust size. Then cut two from the fabric. The seam will be in center front. Cut a curve on the bottom (Fig. 1) as shown. Sew up seam. Turn right side out. Sew a yarn loop at top. The seam was often covered with decoration. Sew on beading or a narrow decorative

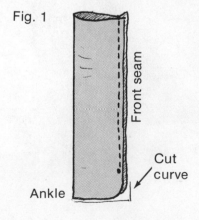

Fig. 1
Front seam
Ankle
Cut curve

strip, if desired. Do not fringe. Cut a piece of yarn or string for waist. Lay breechclout between legs (Fig. 2) with cord over. Slide on leggings, with seam in front. Put string through the loops as shown. Tie string and fold ends of breechclout down (Fig. 3). Leggings should just touch the ground in back. If too long, shorten loop on top. Make moccasins the same as women's. This was all a man wore for everyday.

Kilt: For special occasions, a kilt was added. Measure from knee to waist. Wrap strip of paper this wide around hips and overlap 1/2". Cut fabric this size. Tie around waist (Fig. 4) and fold down top edge. Adjust length—end of breechclout should show below. Kilts were usually decorated with quillwork, beadwork, or fringes. Tie on a yarn sash (Fig. 5).

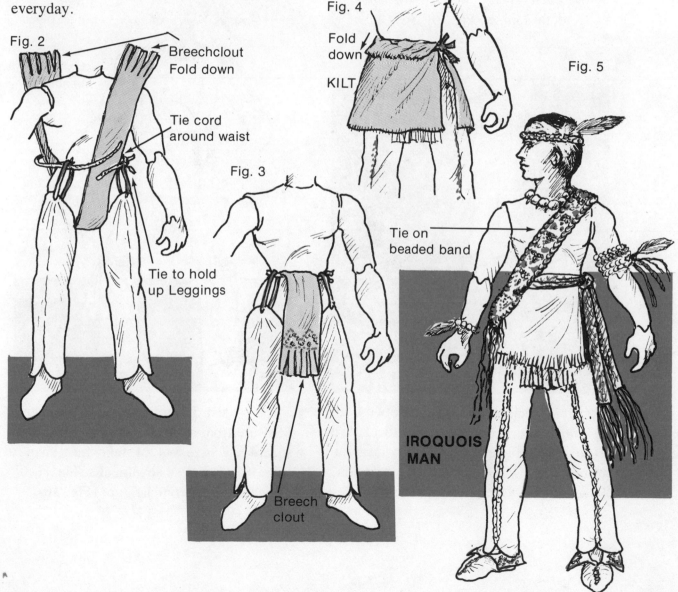

Fig. 2

Breechclout Fold down

Tie cord around waist

Tie to hold up Leggings

Fig. 3

Breech clout

Fig. 4

Fold down

KILT

Fig. 5

Tie on beaded band

IROQUOIS MAN

CHIPPEWA MAN:

Breechclout and moccasins were similar, but their leggings had seams at the side and often were not sewn. Sides were merely tied in several places and held with a garter. Make pattern and cut leggings with straight bottom, turn seam to side and sew in two places. Braid yarns and tie below each knee, allowing the ends to hang to the ankle (Fig. 6). Instead of a

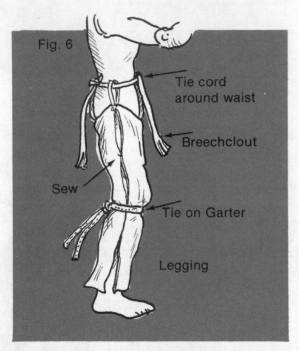

Fig. 6

Tie cord around waist

Breechclout

Sew

Tie on Garter

Legging

Fig. 7

APRON

(Fig. 7). Sew or glue on yarn or felt edging and add beadwork design. Tie on doll (Fig. 8).

Fig. 8

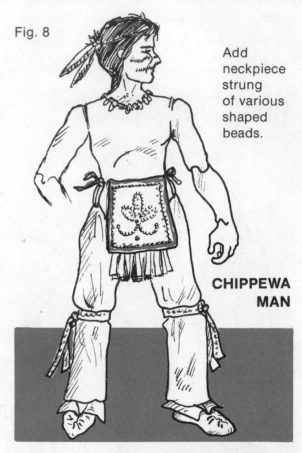

Add neckpiece strung of various shaped beads.

CHIPPEWA MAN

kilt, for special occasions, they wore an apronlike piece tied front and back. To make, measure doll from side to side at the waist. Cut two squares this dimension. Sew or glue yarn across the top for ties

Add a fur robe for cold weather. Measure from ankle to top of head. Cut a square this size out of fake fur. Shape (Fig. 9) to look like an animal's skin, such as bear. Drape around figure (Fig. 10).

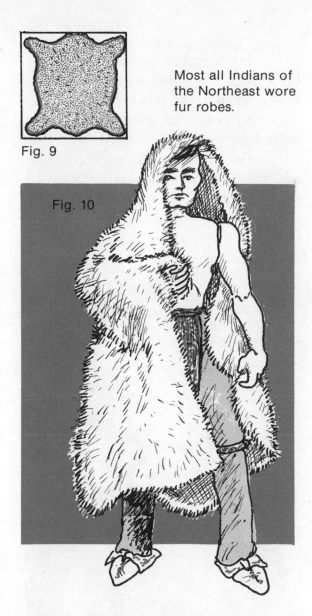

Fig. 9

Most all Indians of the Northeast wore fur robes.

Fig. 10

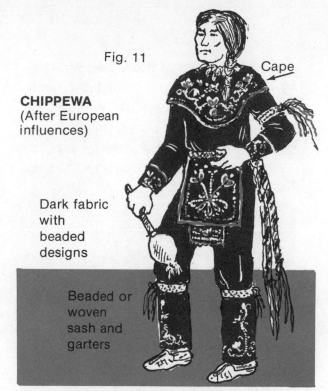

Fig. 11

CHIPPEWA
(After European influences)

Cape

Dark fabric with beaded designs

Beaded or woven sash and garters

The men of the Chippewa and other tribes wore beaded capes or vests for ceremonial occasions. For a cape, make a paper pattern, try on. Cut of fabric (Fig. 12). Add decorations or fringes (Fig. 13).

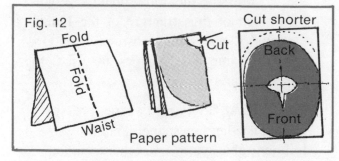

Fig. 12

Fold

Fold

Waist

Cut

Paper pattern

Cut shorter

Back

Front

ALTERNATES: After trade goods were available, clothing for ceremonies became more elaborate, often heavily beaded. Leggings and apron could be made of a dark fabric with beading or decorative tapes sewn on. (Fig. 11).

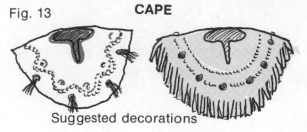

Fig. 13   **CAPE**

Suggested decorations

Add string of beads on a girl (Fig. 14). Make beadwork on a bead loom. Bead a headband about 1/8″ wide or bead belt or garters to fit. For an Iroquois man, bead a sash about 1/2″ wide; tie across chest or around waist (see Fig. 5, page 45).

Fig. 14

String seed and bugle (long) beads. Tie on.

INDIAN COSTUMES

Dressing the dolls should give you some idea of the structure of the Indian clothing. If you want a costume for yourself, the same basic shapes are used, to your measurements.

MATERIALS: Fabric, tape measure, thread, needle, newspapers, masking tape, foil pan, glue, yarn, and other trimmings.

For fabric, use tan cotton such as flannel, suedecloth, or dye an old sheet a tan color. Tape together old newspapers to form pieces large enough to make patterns.

For leggings, measure your jeans or cut legs from a discarded pair and dye brown. Breechclout should be about 9″ or 10″ wide, as long as you are high. Wear tights beneath.

For a girl, measure distance the same as you did for the doll. Draw on paper and try on. Then cut out of fabric. For an Iroquois girl, you can make a dark skirt edged with white beaded design and wear a short print dress on top (Fig. 1).

IROQUOIS
(After European influences)

Fig. 1

Beadwork can be added with markers or really beaded. Designs are suggested throughout the book. Other trims can be added, such as rows of hanging thongs. Make of yarn or cord, threaded on a large-eyed needle. Sew through fabric and add bead (Fig. 2). Or

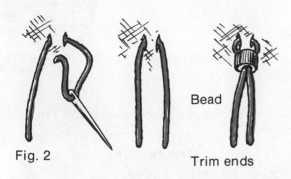

Bead

Fig. 2

Trim ends

dangle cones. Cut shape (Fig. 3) from aluminum foil pan. Roll around pencil (Fig. 4). Knot end of piece of yarn (Fig. 5), slide through and sew on. Rows of cords or jingles were used to decorate yokes or skirt edges (Fig. 6).

Fig. 3

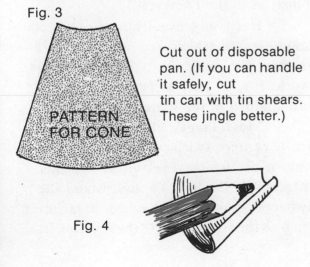

PATTERN FOR CONE

Cut out of disposable pan. (If you can handle it safely, cut tin can with tin shears. These jingle better.)

Fig. 4

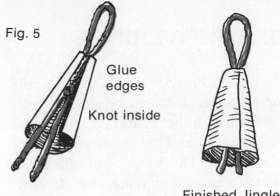

Fig. 5

Glue edges

Knot inside

Finished Jingle

Other decorative techniques described in Chapter 4 can be used to embellish costumes—a dress, kilt or apron.

Fig. 6

CHIPPEWA

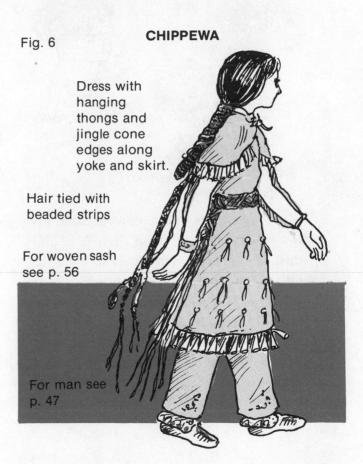

Dress with hanging thongs and jingle cone edges along yoke and skirt.

Hair tied with beaded strips

For woven sash see p. 56

For man see p. 47

HEADCOVERINGS

The headdress or hat was usually for ceremonial dances or other rituals. For warmth in winter, a robe was pulled up around the head, or fur hoods were worn. The whole skin of a small animal was used to make a hat. In some tribes a woven sash was twined around the head like a turban.

Roach

Fabric Hood
beaded design
in white (Micmac)

Algonquian Headcoverings

Turban

Fur on frame,
beaded edge

Animal skin

Warriors spent considerable effort removing hair from their face and most of the head. Hair was scraped off with a sharp stone or pulled out or singed with a hot stick. Only a tuft of hair, the scalp lock, was left. Older men and nonwarriors (such as priests) wore their hair long and straight. For special occasions, a crest of dyed deer hair (roach) was fitted over and tied onto the scalp lock to augment the style. These stiff deer hairs, sewn onto a leather base, stood straight up, and a tall feather was often added.

Each tribe had distinctive head-dresses. The Chippewa made a crown of feathers (crest), which fanned vertically from front to back. An Iroquois crown had large feathers set upright in a base. Generally, feathers were not used as much as in the Far West.

Hats were usually made over a splint frame which was covered with leather, fur, or fabric. A band of bead-work, fur, or later punched metal was often added to the bottom edge.

Most large, standing, single feathers were twirlers, a feather fitted onto a pin which revolved in a socket attached to the hat. To understand the twirlers, make one attached to a hat such as the Gustoweah ("the real hat").

Hats (old Iroquois drawing)

Iroquois Hat (Gustoweah)

MATERIALS: Gallon-size plastic bottle (milk, bleach, etc.), spool (nonwood), one large-holed, 3/8″-diameter bead, one round toothpick, 12″ feather, about 30 feathers 4″ or 5″ long (preferably pre-strung), felt or durable fabric about 9″ x 24″, buttonhole thread and needle, sewing thread and needle, small piece of fake fur, 24″ piece of 3/4″ woven decorative tape or beadwork, glue. Heavy scissors, Sobo glue, awl, sandpaper, tissue paper, masking tape.

First construct the framework for the hat. Authentically, the frame should be made of splint or leather, but the same effect can be achieved more easily and at no cost with a plastic bottle. Make sure the bottle is clean. Cut off the bottom. Mark dimensions shown: a 1½″ bottom band and four vertical tabs spaced equally apart (Fig. 1). Cut as shown. Cut a 1″ strip from a leftover piece of plastic to complete the tab on side where handle prevented cutting a full-length tab. With awl, poke two holes through both pieces (Fig. 2). Tie tab in place using heavy thread. Overlap three

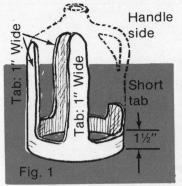

of the vertical tabs (Fig. 3) and tape to hold. Try on. It should fit loosely. If too tight, insert a piece in base. Make holes and tie together (Fig. 4).

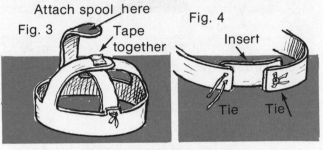

To make the twirling feather, use a small-size, foam-type spool from sewing thread. Whittle, enlarging the hole in one end (Fig. 5). Push toothpick into bead and break off small protruding tip. Remove, add glue, and push back into bead, attaching securely. Push tip of the 12″ feather down on projecting pointed tip of toothpick (Fig. 6). Trim end, if needed. Remove feather and set aside. Place bead in

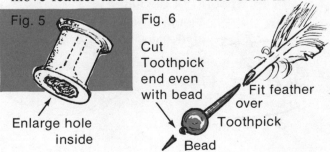

whittled end of spool, point up, and check that it revolves freely. Now, sew base of spool to the free tab, using buttonhole thread (Fig. 7).

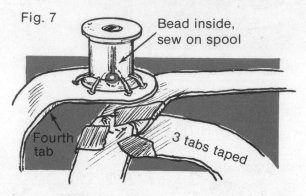

Fig. 7

Bead inside, sew on spool

Fourth tab

3 tabs taped

After attaching the spool, curve end down over other three tabs. Poke holes with awl. Sew all four pieces together, with spool on top, to complete the framework (Fig. 8).

For hat covering, measure 1/4 of area. Add 3/8″ seam all around. Cut pattern out of paper and lay over frame (Fig. 9). Check to make sure each section is large enough and doesn't fit too tight. When pattern is satisfactory, cut four out of felt or fabric.

Pin together, wrong side out, onto frame (Fig. 10); adjust as needed. Sew up

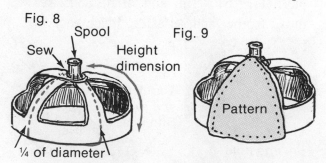

Fig. 8

Sew

Spool

Height dimension

¼ of diameter

Fig. 9

Pattern

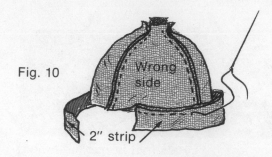

Fig. 10

Wrong side

2″ strip

seams. Cut a 2″ strip long enough to go around the bottom of the frame. Place right sides together and sew to bottom edge of hat fabric. Turn right side out and fit onto frame. Trim top opening to fit around spool. Fold bottom strip to inside around frame and sew. Sew or glue decorative tape, ribbon or beadwork around bottom edge.

Cover top of hat with rows of shorter feathers. Some suppliers (see back of book) carry feathers already strung for this purpose. If you buy loose feathers, thread a sewing needle and push through the end of each feather (Fig. 11). Lay feathers on the hat so that ends are above the decorative strip. Mark a line (Fig. 12). With another thread, sew the feathers to the fabric (Fig. 13). Add glue if needed to hold. String another row of feathers and repeat, placing it near the top and overlapping the first row (Fig. 14). Sew in place.

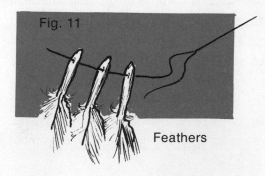

Fig. 11

Feathers

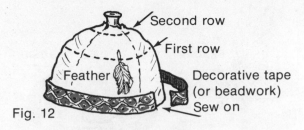

Fig. 12

— Second row
— First row
Feather
Decorative tape (or beadwork)
Sew on

Cut piece of fur about 1½" x 7". Sew a running stitch along one edge and pull up. Add glue to spool and attach fur

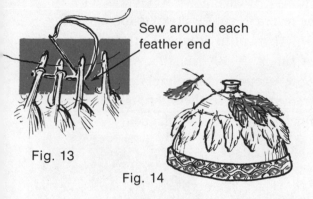

Sew around each feather end

Fig. 13

Fig. 14

around spool. Edge should overlap ends of last row of feathers (Fig. 15). Or wind fluffy yarn around and glue end.

Add a little glue to tip of 12" feather and insert in spool, onto the pointed tip of a toothpick (Fig. 16). It should twirl.

Fig. 15
Spool
Fur
Feathers

Fig. 16
Feather

THE "GUSTOWEAH"

ALTERNATES: Hat can be made of paper if you can't invest in feathers. Make the frame, then cut a piece of crepe paper about 10" x 24". Gather paper around the spool, add glue, and tie (Fig. 17). Trim even with top of spool. Fold up bottom around frame to inside and glue. Cut paper feathers (Fig. 18) and add dark coloring on tips with markers. Glue on two rows. Color a paper strip to look like beading and glue to edge. Wind yarn around top. Cut a big paper feather, insert, and glue into spool hole (Fig. 19).

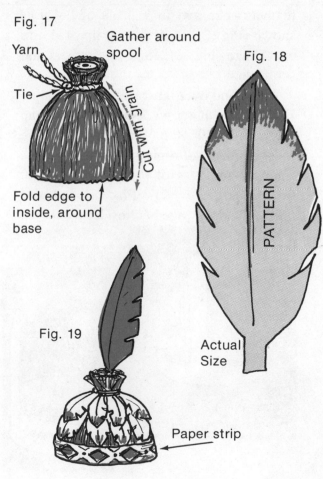

Fig. 17
Gather around spool
Yarn
Tie
Cut with grain
Fold edge to inside, around base

Fig. 18
PATTERN
Actual Size

Fig. 19
Paper strip

Chippewa Hat

MATERIALS: Gallon-size plastic container, scrap fabric or thin piece of foam rubber, fake fur (preferably brown), two feathers about 7″ or 8″, yarn or other trims, awl, sewing thread, needle, thimbles.

A similar frame is needed for this hat. Cut bottle, this time making only two vertical tabs, each about 1″ wide (Fig. 1). They must be opposite each other. Punch two holes midway between tabs on each side. To make a secure slot for each feather, poke awl in and out of holes as shown (Fig. 2). Push feather tip in slot to check size (Fig. 3). Remove feathers and set aside.

Bend over tabs, overlap, and tape. For padding under fur, cut a piece of scrap fabric about 10″ × 20″ and roll up. If using foam rubber, cut a piece about 20″ × 1″. Tape around base of frame (Fig. 4). Cut fake fur strip 3″ × 21″. Place around base and sew edges together inside, as shown

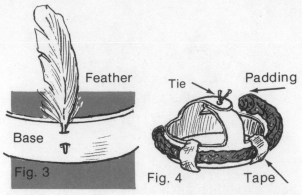

Fig. 3 — Feather, Base

Fig. 4 — Tie, Padding, Tape

(Fig. 5). Sew across and pull together firmly. At each place where a feather will be inserted, cut fur down to top edge (Fig. 6). Also cut in at tabs. Cut another piece of fur 3″ × 10″ and fit over center tabs. Sew around, completely covering the frame. Insert feathers through slits in the fur and into slots as planned.

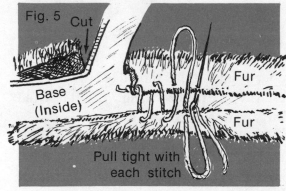

Fig. 5 — Cut, Base (Inside), Fur, Fur, Pull tight with each stitch

Hats often had hanging fur cords either over each shoulder or in back. For a tail, cut a piece of fur 3½″ × 10″. Sew, folding edges together. Sew to back of hat

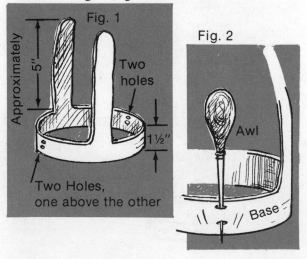

Fig. 1 — Approximately 5″, Two holes, 1½″, Two Holes, one above the other

Fig. 2 — Awl, Base

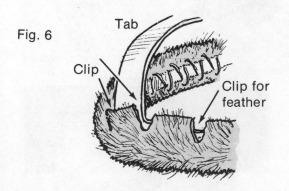

Fig. 6 — Tab, Clip, Clip for feather

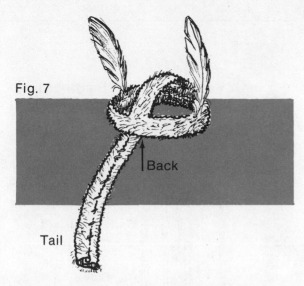

Fig. 7

Back

Tail

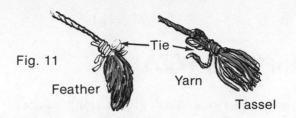

Fig. 11

Tie

Feather

Yarn

Tassel

(Fig. 7). Metal cones were often attached to end of tail or along edges, or thimbles were substituted. Use three cheap thimbles. Poke hole in end of each with awl (Fig. 8). Push yarn through the hole, tie a knot (Fig. 9), and pull up into thimble. Sew yarn to tail, placing thimbles at slightly different lengths; they should hit each other (Fig. 10).

Instead of a fur tail, braid some yarn 20″ long. Fold in half and sew middle to hat. At ends of the yarn, add small, fluffy feathers. Add glue to feather tip, wind yarn around several times, and glue

end (Fig. 11), or add yarn tassels.

This type of hat was also worn by women but without any standing feathers (Fig. 12).

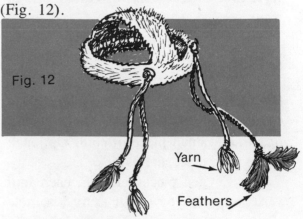

Fig. 12

Yarn

Feathers

ALTERNATES: This frame can be a firm foundation for a feathered headdress. Make tabs side to side. Poke holes with awl (see Fig. 2) at proper angles to position feathers and create the effect desired (Fig. 13). Cover frame with fabric, fur, or a beaded band.

Fig. 8

Awl

Thimble

Fig. 9

Fig. 10

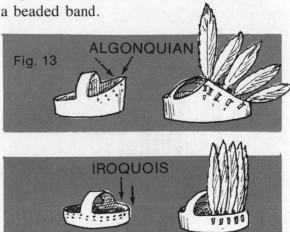

Fig. 13

ALGONQUIAN

IROQUOIS

FINGER WEAVING

Various natural materials were used for finger weaving of sashes and straps. By 1850 most all were made with yarn. Finger-woven sashes are back in style today; here is how to make one to wear.

Sash

MATERIALS: At least three colors of rug or other heavy yarn, stick (dowel, pencil, or stirrer), small piece of cord. Optional: cardboard, tape, and T-pins.

Cut ten pieces of yarn, each four yards long. If you prefer to try a sample piece—such as a bookmark—cut eight pieces of yarn, one yard each. Fold each piece in half, lay over the stick, arranging colors in groups. Tie a short piece of cord to the ends of the stick (Fig. 1). Fasten the cord to a firm support.

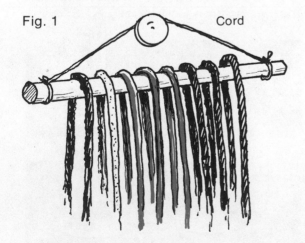

Fig. 1   Cord

Or work on a board. Tape together two layers of corrugated cardboard. Use macramé T-pins to hold stick and yarn onto the board as weaving progresses (Fig. 2).

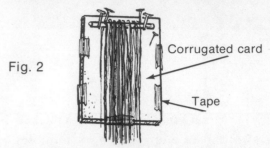

Fig. 2   Corrugated card

Tape

TO WEAVE: Each strand on the left will, in turn, weave under and over to the right, then become a vertical strand to be woven in with the rest.

Pick up each strand below the stick, letting the strands over the stick lay below, alternating in order in your hand. Now, pick up the first strand on the left and bring it across to the right, laying it between the strands you are holding apart (Fig. 3). Pin this first strand, or lay it up over the stick so it won't get confused with the others (Fig. 4).

For the next row, pick up outside strand on the left and bring it to the right

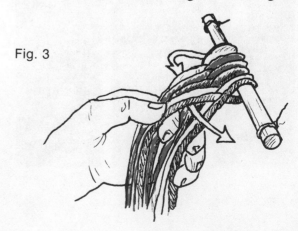

Fig. 3

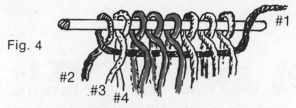

Fig. 4

#1

#2

#3 #4

so it goes alternately under and over, opposite to the previous row (Fig. 5). Take the first strand that was put up (#1 on drawing), lay down and put #2 strand up over rod. First strand now becomes part of

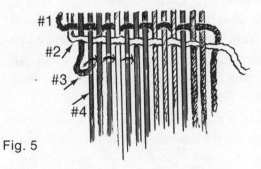

#1

#2

#3

#4

Fig. 5

the weaving (Fig. 6). Continue weaving by repeating this process, alternating over and under. Last strand on right must follow also; over or under, as needed. Push woven strands close together. Color will zig-zag across the weaving (Fig. 7).

When piece is long enough for your purpose, tie ends, knotting two cords

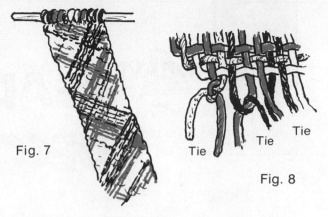

Fig. 7

Tie   Tie   Tie   Tie

Fig. 8

together (Fig. 8). Slip top off the stick, cut and tie yarn (Fig. 9). If desired, add extra yarn for sash ties. Tie yarn piece into each loop making a fringe (Fig. 10).

Fig. 9

Cut   Cut

Stick Removed

Tie   Top edge

Fig. 10

Tie in extra yarn

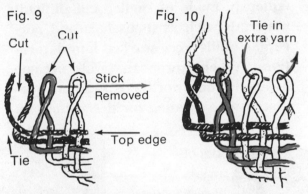

ALTERNATES: Beads can be added as weaving progresses. Or add in fringe, knotting below each bead (Fig. 11).

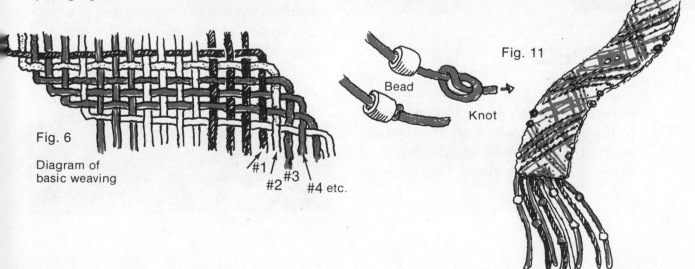

Fig. 6

Diagram of basic weaving

#1 #3
#2   #4 etc.

Fig. 11

Bead   Knot

4 BEADS AND OTHER DECORATIONS

It seems incredible that the Indians had time to decorate their possessions, since making the essentials took so much work. Yet beads were tediously made of shells, and difficult materials such as moosehair and porcupine quills were worked into decorations. When European beads became available, quillwork was gradually replaced with beading for decorations on leather or fabric.

Iroquois

White beads on dark fabric

Floral, some color in later examples

Algonquian

WAMPUM

The origins of beadmaking are very ancient. Coastal Indians made beads of shells found on the Atlantic beaches. These beads, and the strings or belts made from them, were called *wampunoeag*, an Algonquian word, later shortened to *wampum*. The outside of welk or similar shell was knocked away, leaving a core that was then cut into pieces, shaped and polished. A hole was drilled. These were the white beads. Purple beads were shaped in the same way from certain clam shells that have a small purple area. The purples were rarer than the white and therefore more valuable.

Despite the fact that shells were very hard, the Indians made wampum from them without using metal tools. Each bead was about 8mm × 4mm. The beads were worn on strings or woven into strips. At first wampum was probably worn for decoration, but gradually it came to have particular meanings and special values.

By the time the Europeans arrived, wampum had significance in

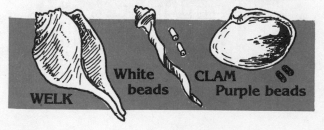

WELK   White beads   CLAM   Purple beads

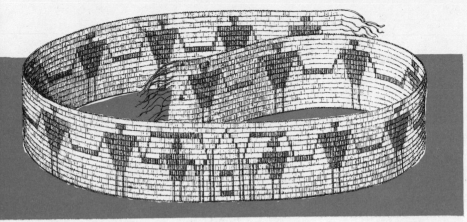

Onondaga wampum belt made of nearly 10,000 shell beads. It is believed to have been made to record a treaty.

many areas. Inland Indians exchanged or traded for wampum. A messenger carried a wampum string to identify himself. A white string meant good fortune; purple, sorrow or anger; if dabbed with red, war. Strings of beads could be a gift to a family—for a bride or as payment for killing a family member.

Official wampum was woven into a strip or "belt," usually the length of a man's reach and as much as 4″ wide. At meetings, a tribal leader held a wampum belt as he spoke, as a sign of his authority. Special wampum belts were made to convey a message, commemorate an alliance, or make a treaty binding.

The designs woven into the strips were like documents recording events. A special member of each tribe was trained to memorize the meanings. The history of the tribe was thus preserved and important events recorded. The Europeans, noting the Indian's respect for wampum, assigned it money value, and used it as money.

The Indian women wove belts on a bow loom. To understand how it was done, try a small practice piece.

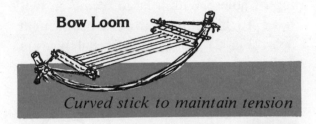

Bow Loom

Curved stick to maintain tension

Wampum Weaving

MATERIALS: Tubetti (#41 size about 1/4″ long, 3/16″ diameter), string or thin twine (waxed linen for macramé is excellent), sewing thread, two needles that will go through your beads (preferably with blunt ends), foam-type supermarket tray, stick about 6″ long, small dish, purple dye, paper towels. Optional: bleach.

To color Tubetti, mix a small amount of purple dye. When cool, add Tubetti. Do not soak. Lift out of dye with slotted spoon or stick. Dry on paper towels. For white, use natural color or place in a diluted solution of bleach for a few seconds and place on paper towel in the sun.

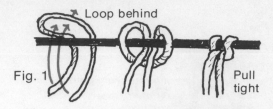

Fig. 1   Loop behind   Pull tight

Fig. 4

Decide on length of wampum. 8" is good for a sample piece. Add 8" extra. Cut eight cords twice the length needed (32"). Tie the middle of each cord onto the stick (Fig. 1).

For spacers, cut two pieces, each 1" × 5", from foam tray or card. Measure average length of beads to determine spacing of holes. With a large needle or awl, poke 16 holes in a row, a bead-length apart (Fig. 2). Poke cords through holes in

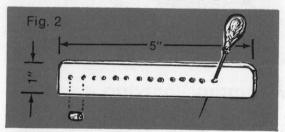

Fig. 2   ← 5" →   1"

order and bring first spacer up near stick. Repeat for other spacer, keeping cords in order (Fig. 3). Tie cords together at the end below the spacer. Tie an extra piece of cord onto the stick at the top.

Cords must be kept taut. Tie between two firm supports such as a knob and a chair back. Move chair as needed to keep proper tension in cords (Fig. 4) as you work.

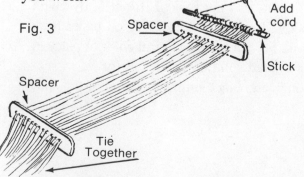

Fig. 3   Spacer   Add cord   Stick

Spacer   Tie Together

To bead, use design shown (Fig. 5). Each square represents a bead. (Or plot out a design of your own on graph paper.) Thread two needles and tie ends together. One needle goes across below the cords, the other above. On one needle, thread 15

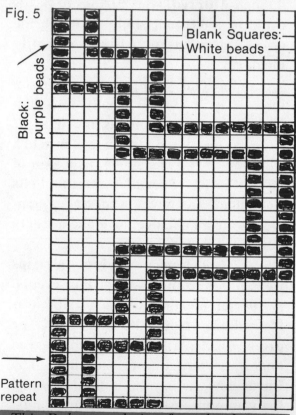

Fig. 5

Black: purple beads

Blank Squares: White beads

Pattern repeat

This Delaware design for a land treaty may have represented hills and valleys or indicated the Indians right to continue to travel across the lands he sold.

of the proper color beads (see graph). Go under cords and push beads up between cords with finger (Fig. 6). Now bring second needle through this row of beads, going over each cord. Each bead will have two threads going through, thus holding it

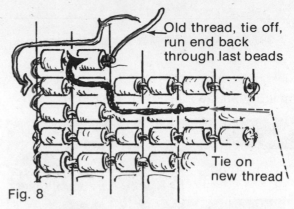

Old thread, tie off, run end back through last beads

Tie on new thread

Fig. 8

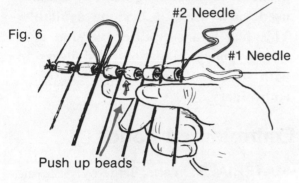

Fig. 6

#2 Needle

#1 Needle

Push up beads

firmly in place between the cords (Fig. 7).

Go around the end cord and go back, attaching the beads for the next row. Repeat and continue in this manner. Push each row up against previous row.

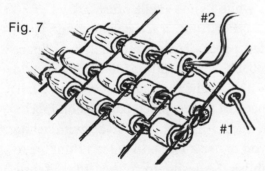

Fig. 7

#2

#1

When thread runs short, tie it to cord and run ends under a couple of adjacent beads. Cut off. Thread needle, tie on new end, and run through two or three beads, coming out at the place where you need to continue work (Fig. 8). It is pref-

erable to tie on new threads near the middle rather than at the edges to keep the edges neat.

When complete, untie the bottom cords and remove spacer. Tie cord ends in pairs. Break off top spacer. Hang up (Fig. 9).

ALTERNATES: Weaving could be any width or length. A belt might be 10 cords wide. Use this method to make multicolor

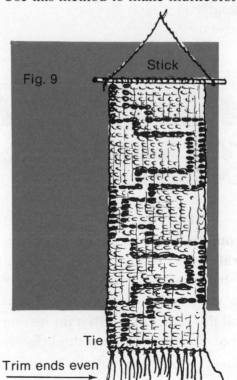

Fig. 9

Stick

Tie

Trim ends even

designs using tube- or tile-size beads or make your own beads of paper (Fig. 10).

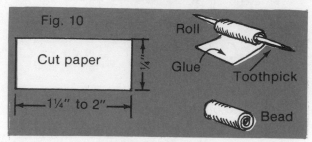

A bow loom (trade name "Beaderette Loom") is available in some craft shops from Artis, Inc. (See list of suppliers). Any inexpensive bead loom (Fig. 11) could be used for a narrow piece.

If you wish to make a more durable piece, authentic wampum-type beads are available from Plume Trading (see suppliers). Such beads are expensive, however.

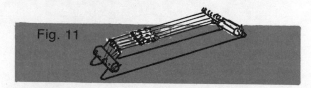

MOOSEHAIR EMBROIDERY

The Woodland Indians used hair from the mane of a moose to make decorations on leather. These hairs, about 5″ long, took dye well. Several were laid on the surface and tacked down. We call this couching. Often the leather was dyed dark to show up the brightly col-ored hairs. For another effect, bunches of hair were pulled up from the underside and trimmed into tufts.

With yarn, you can get the moosehair look without having the problem of short lengths. The Indians used yarn when it became available. This bag is a simplified version of a Huron pouch made of dyed deerskin with deer hair fringe and moosehair embroidery.

Embroidered Pouch

MATERIALS: Yarn, large-eyed needle (to hold yarn), sewing thread and needle, black felt or velvet (about 9″ × 14″), 1/2″ wide black ribbon, embroidery floss, 8″ embroidery hoop, paper, chalk, white crayon, Sobo glue. Optional: waxed paper, white paint, small brush.

For front, trace design (Fig. 1) on folded paper. Trace other half and open. For back, draw outline of front and add flap. Draw other half and open. Rub chalk on back of paper, place patterns on fabric, and trace (Fig. 2). Go over with white crayon or use a brush to paint a thin line to establish the design to follow. Place fabric on embroidery hoop.

Decide on colors, such as red and white with accents of blue and orange. Persian yarn or yarn of a similar thickness is best. Embroidery floss (full six strands) can be used for accent colors.

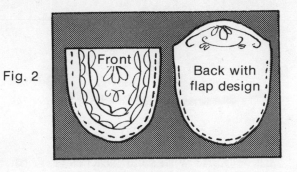

Fig. 2 Front — Back with flap design

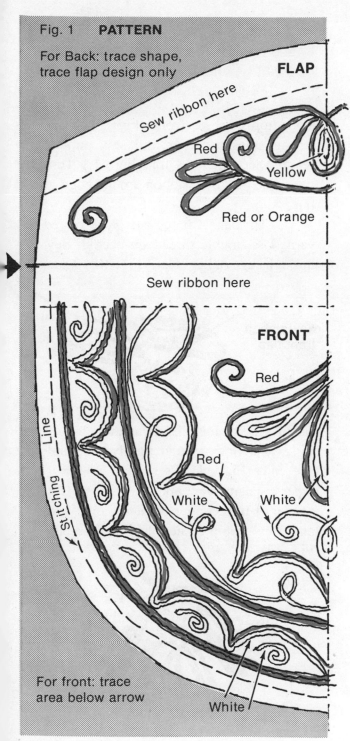

Fig. 1 PATTERN

For Back: trace shape, trace flap design only

FLAP

Sew ribbon here

Red

Yellow

Red or Orange

Sew ribbon here

FRONT

Red

Stitching Line

Red

White

White

White

For front: trace area below arrow

Cut a piece of yarn 5″ or 6″ larger than area it will cover in design. Thread yarn on large needle. Thread sewing needle with thread to match yarn, if possible. Poke yarn needle up from the back at start of line of design. Pull through, leaving a short end in back. Knot end of sewing thread and bring out on drawn line near yarn (Fig. 3). Lay yarn along drawn

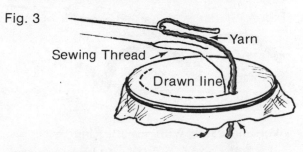

Fig. 3 Yarn — Sewing Thread — Drawn line

line, then insert sewing needle on drawn line again, going over the yarn (Fig. 4). Bring sewing needle out again not more than 1/8″ further along the drawn line. Go over yarn and repeat (Fig. 5), attaching

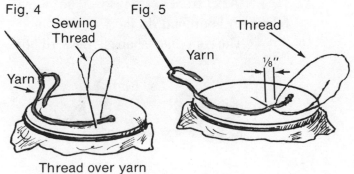

Fig. 4 Sewing Thread — Yarn

Fig. 5 Thread — Yarn — 1/8″

Thread over yarn

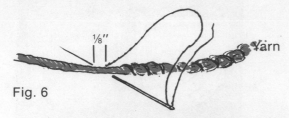

Fig. 6

Fig. 9

Sew on ribbon

yarn to fabric with small stitches (Fig. 6).

When one color of the design is completed, use yarn needle again to bring yarn out in back. Cut off, leaving a short end. Knot sewing thread behind and cut off. Start new part of pattern with new color and repeat.

For small motifs, go behind with yarn, come out again at next motif, and continue (Fig. 7). For loops, twist yarn

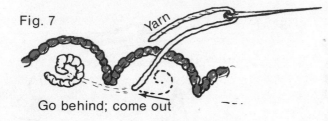

Fig. 7

Yarn

Go behind; come out

over and catch with sewing (Fig. 8).

If you have difficulty keeping yarn in place, it might help to glue it slightly. Run a thin line of glue along drawn line. Lay on yarn, lay piece of wax paper on top, and press down. Allow to dry, then sew as before.

After front design is worked, move fabric on hoop and do the flap design.

Cut out bag shapes. Sew ribbon

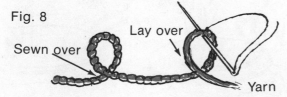

Fig. 8

Lay over

Sewn over

Yarn

along top edge of front (Fig. 9). Place wrong sides together and sew outside seam. (See stitching line Fig. 1.) Turn right side out. Sew ribbon around edge of flap.

To make fringe, cut piece of red yarn. Use double thread on needle. Sew through edge of bag. Cut. (Fig. 10.) Add a

Fig. 10

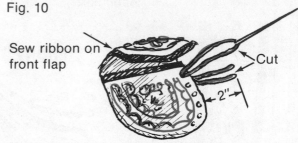

Sew ribbon on front flap

Cut

2"

dab of glue to the yarn near the edge of bag. Wind floss around tightly, tie, and glue ends (Fig. 11). Press until it sticks. Repeat, spacing yarn about 1/4″ apart. Cut a piece of ribbon approximately one yard long. Sew to top corners to complete bag (Fig. 12).

Fig. 11

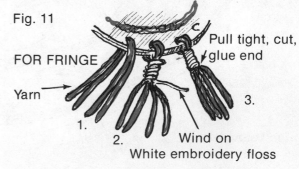

FOR FRINGE

Yarn

Pull tight, cut, glue end

1.

2.

3.

Wind on White embroidery floss

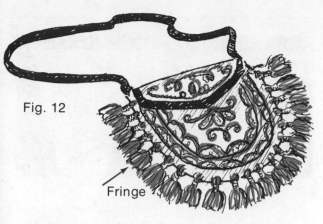

Fig. 12

Fringe

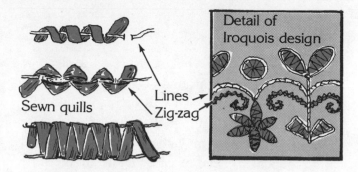

Sewn quills

Lines
Zig-zag

Detail of
Iroquois design

ALTERNATES: The couching technique can also be used to get an effect of sewn beadwork. Rattail is a satin cord sold in craft shops for macramé and jewelry. Couch the rattail to tan or dark fabric instead of yarn. The area between each stitch shines like a bead. Plastic raffia, couched, looks like a type of quillwork.

QUILLWORK

In areas where porcupines were plentiful, exquisite designs were made with quills. Working with porcupine quills was an Indian innovation, done no other place in the world. The quills were cleaned, dyed, soaked, and flattened in preparation. The women devised many methods of attaching quills to leather surfaces. A few simple techniques are shown here. Quills were also worked on rawhide cords to be applied to hard surfaces and wrapping methods used.

When wet, a quill softens; when dry it is hard and shiny, giving a sheen to the design. Pouches, cases, mocca-sins, pipe stems, ceremonial garments, cradle boards, and household goods were decorated. For birchbark boxes, ends of porcupine quills were bent and inserted into holes punched in the bark. A birchbark lining was added to cover and hold them in place.

It took great patience and skill to work the quills. There is no substitute today for this work, and it's unlikely you'll ever get a chance to work with real porcupine quills. However, it is fun to try some of the techniques used.

A Delaware knife sheath, decorated with various quilled designs and edged with a deer hair fringe was the inspiration for the project below: an attractive case for one of your most useful tools, scissors.

Scissors Sheath

MATERIALS: Scissors (4″ to 6″ long), felt, lightweight card, plastic drinking straws (at least two colors), buttonhole thread and sewing thread (colors to match felt it possible), needles, masking tape, glue, pins, yarn, or raffia. Optional: beads.

Pattern: Lay your scissors on a piece of paper. Draw around scissors, adding 3/8" as shown (Fig. 1). Cut out paper and fold in half (Fig. 2) to make sure both sides are the same. Trim and open. Draw around paper on piece of card. Draw another line on card 3/16" inside drawn line. Cut card along inside line. This is your pattern.

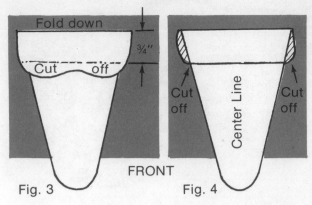

Fig. 3   FRONT   Fig. 4

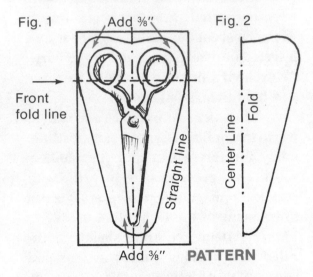

Fig. 1   Add ⅜"   Fig. 2

Front fold line

Straight line

Center Line   Fold

Add ⅜"   **PATTERN**

Using tan or brown felt, place your pattern so that you can cut three. Take two felt pieces and glue one to either side of the card, covering front and back. For front, take third piece and fold down on the dotted line shown in Fig. 1. Cut flap straight across 3/4" below dotted line (Fig. 3). Trim corners to match edges (Fig. 4). Design will be applied to front piece.

Select a plain color straw (not striped), and press flat so that it cracks along edges. Cut into strips about 1/8" or 3/16" wide. Cut two pieces of buttonhole

thread about 15" long and tie ends together. Tie another knot about 1 ½" below (Fig. 5). Tie ends to a desk knob or other firm support and insert end of strip of straw between cord. Tape to hold temporarily (Fig. 5).

The following process is similar to braiding: Fold straw strip, angling down and under thread (Fig. 5). Fold over thread and bring to other side (Fig. 6). Lay thread over strip, fold plastic over thread and back to other side (Fig. 7). Lay thread over, fold, and repeat. Straw strip should fold at angle, threads remain straight about 1/8" or 3/16" apart as parallel as possible (Fig. 8). Thread will be covered, showing a bit only at intersections.

Fig. 5   Fig. 6   Fig. 7

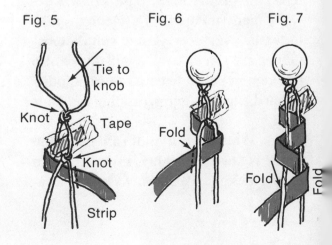

Tie to knob

Knot   Tape

Knot

Fold

Fold

Fold

Strip

When straw strip is finished, fold a piece of tape around end to hold. Cut strip off the knob. Make three strips for the front of sheath and two across the folded-down flap (see Fig. 15). Decide on your color arrangement and braid the strips needed.

Mark center line on felt and place center strip. With sewing thread and needle, come up from behind and through the felt, between the buttonhole thread and fold of straw strip (Fig. 9). Go back in on other side of buttonhole thread at the same spot. Go across behind and come out at corner of fold on other edge of strip (Fig. 10). Go back in and continue, sewing down at each fold corner (Fig. 11). When complete, sewing hardly shows. At the bottom end, fold straw strip and threads

behind and sew over to secure (Fig. 12). Trim off any excess.

Thread large needle, with buttonhold thread at the top of the strip and sew through to back. Tie threads in back and clip off ends. Top ends of straw strip will be hidden under flap.

Sew a strip on either side of center strip, repeating the process. For a larger scissor's sheath, add another row each side, making five strips on front. Sew two or three strips across the flap, making sure it is on the folded-down side of the flap. Fold ends under on each side to secure.

Add couched designs (see page 64), if desired. Quills were often couched on for outline designs. Use a bright color, natural or mat raffia. Draw a wavy line on either side of strips (Fig. 13). Couch in place. Make an edge line along strip and lines on flap, if desired.

Assemble sheath. Place front on the back, fold flap down, position, and pin. Using raffia or yarn and a large-eyed

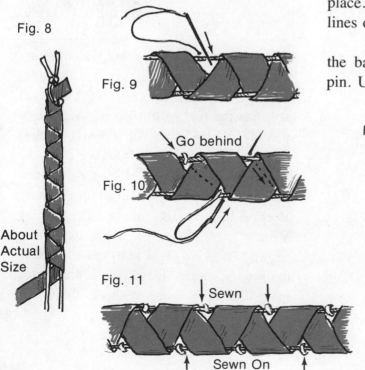

Fig. 8

Fig. 9

Fig. 10

Go behind

Fig. 11

About Actual Size

Sewn

Sewn On

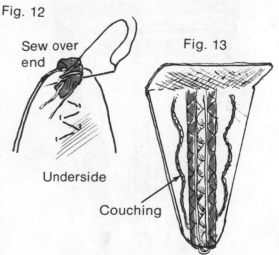

Fig. 12

Sew over end

Underside

Fig. 13

Couching

67

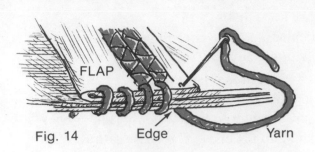

FLAP   Edge   Yarn

Fig. 14

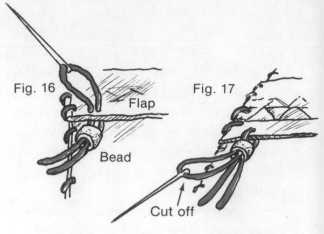

Fig. 16   Flap   Fig. 17

Bead

Cut off

needle, sew all edges (Fig. 14). Catch in flap. Sew up around top (Fig. 15).

Add some tassels, if desired. Use large-holed beads (ponies). Thread yarn on large needle. Use double. Go through bead; sew through edge of flap (Fig. 16) and back through bead. Cut off (Fig. 17). Repeat, making four tassels (Fig. 18). Add a dab of glue inside the bead if it tends to slip off. Slide scissors into their sheath. If you wish it to hang up, tie a cord or yarn loop to top center.

Braided strips that look like Quillwork, can be used to decorate a bag, moccasins, box, jacket, book cover, or whatever you'd like.

Fig. 15

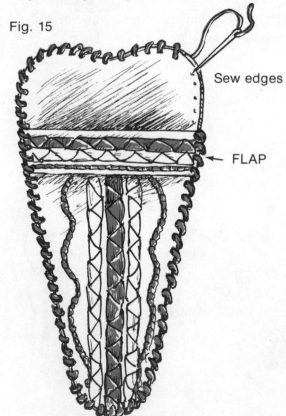

Sew edges

FLAP

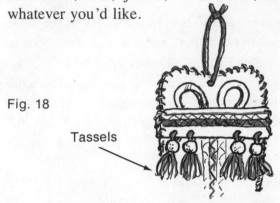

Fig. 18

Tassels

ALTERNATE: If you can't find drinking straws in plain colors, use a substitute, which is actually easier to work and yet still has the feel of quillwork when completed. Cut 1/4″ strips of adhesive-backed vinyl. (Trade names: Contact, Kwik-Kover, Adorn, etc.) Select plain colors, not patterns. Cut each strip about 12″ long. Peel off backing and fold in half, sticking strip to itself (Fig. 19). Work as before, angling folds to get a textured strip. For the row on either side of the center strip, make one strip using a piece about 20″

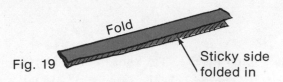

Fig. 19

Fold

Sticky side
folded in

long. Shape folded strip around tip over
end of center strip (Fig. 20) for a neater
point. Sew on strips as before.

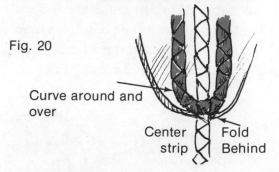

Fig. 20

Curve around and
over

Center
strip

Fold
Behind

Algonquian
beaded
Moccasin toe
(Cree)

BEADWORK

Early beaded designs were simple outlines—usually white beads only. As beads became more available, motifs were filled in. Later, entire surfaces were covered with beads of all colors.

A Mohawk piece made about 1616 is one of the earliest known Indian beadwork examples. Beading did not come to the Great Lakes until about 1700. Most beadwork was done in the eighteenth and nineteenth centuries.

The simple, double-curve designs of the Indians later became more floral, probably influenced by the French. Elaborate florals were worked on dark-colored velvet for ceremonial

Double curve designs

wear. Designs often had special meanings intended to give favor to the wearer.

Bow looms were used for small pieces such as garters, bands, and belts, but most designs were applied to the surface. Two methods were used. Beads were either stitched directly onto the fabric, or overlaid (couched). Couching was better suited to curved designs.

Overlaid Bead Panel

MATERIALS: Seed beads (white and two or three other colors), felt (black or dark blue), embroidery hoop, black thread and needle, monofilament (nylon) fishing line (''6-pound test'' or less), tracing wheel, transfer paper or chalk, small stationery clip, pins, and white crayon (or white paint and small brush).

Draw a design on paper. Trace Fig. 1, a single line for each line of beads. Adapt to fit area you plan to use. Pin pattern on felt, lay transfer paper underneath, and use tracing wheel to transfer pattern. If the guideline is faint, go over with white crayon or use a little paint with a small brush.

Stretch felt on embroidery hoop. Cut a piece of nylon line, knot, and come up from behind. String on a row of beads. Traditionally, beads were strung on a beading needle and thread, but the nylon line eliminates the frustrations of beads with too-small holes. Thread black thread on sewing needle. Tie knot in end. Come up from behind near the same spot and lay beads along line, bringing thread over beads, and go back in almost the same spot. Thread will go between the beads and not show. Work from the top, inserting needle again, under and out. Each time go over nylon line about three beads' distance further along drawn line (Fig. 2).

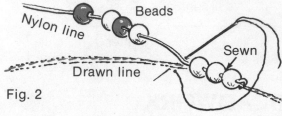

Fig. 2

Continue adding beads (Fig. 3) and catching down with the black thread.

If one-color beads are used for some distance, they can all be strung and then pushed up as needed. Clip end of nylon line to the edge of the fabric to pre-

Fig. 1

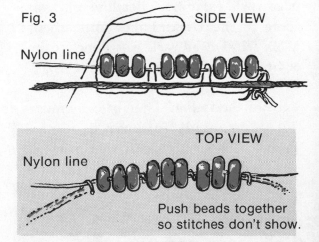

Fig. 3   SIDE VIEW

Nylon line

TOP VIEW

Nylon line

Push beads together so stitches don't show.

70

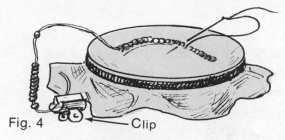

Fig. 4 ← Clip

vent beads from sliding off (Fig. 4).

When one-color area is complete, tie thread and nylon line securely in back. Or carry both behind, over to the next area, and out to front. Slide next color beads on line. Do outline first (Fig. 5), fill in next row right against outline, and continue. Do inside last (Fig. 6). For tight curves, sew between each bead.

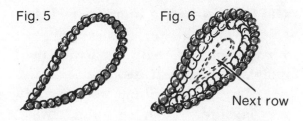

Fig. 5   Fig. 6

Next row

When complete, remove from hoop, turn under edges, and sew onto bag flap, pocket, or for whatever it was planned.

ALTERNATES: Some seed beads come prestrung and can be used as is for part of the design.

Try other beading designs (Fig. 7), adapted from Indian motifs. Draw to fit size needed. Many designs throughout the book may be adapted to beadwork.

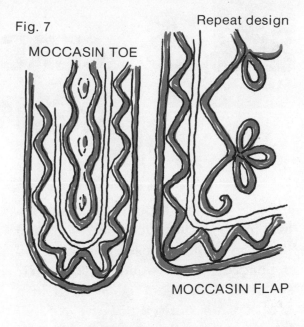

Fig. 7   Repeat design

MOCCASIN TOE

MOCCASIN FLAP

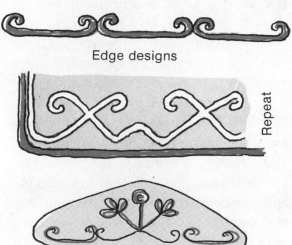

Edge designs

Repeat

Design for headband or collar

Other band or strap designs appear at the beginning of each chapter.

5 CEREMONY AND RELIGION

The Indians' religious beliefs involved the natural forces around them, as they lived close to nature and depended on the woodland for their survival. Although they believed in a great creator spirit, a "Master of Life" presiding over all nature, this was a far distant force and had little to do with their individual lives. The multitudes of spirits dwelling in every natural form were the gods they dealt with.

Everything had a spirit within it: animals, trees, rocks, plants. This presence was always felt and required special homage. A human's spirit could increase by a proper relationship with the spirits of nature. Often this relationship was interpreted through dreams. They believed dreams were messages from gods.

In many tribes a child was given only a temporary name until old enough to receive a rightful name. An animal or other spirit that appeared in a dream might determine the proper name and become a "Totem," a protective guardian spirit.

It was believed that death took a person's being to a peaceful place of plenty, but the spirit stayed with loved ones. People who had departed—the "Old Ones"—were a comfort and help to the living and, they believed, went with warriors into battle or joined the family at special festivals.

Prayers and rituals were part of everyday life. When an animal was killed for food, a piece was left with an explanation to the animal's spirit telling why it had been necessary to kill it. When a tree was cut, or clay removed from the earth to make a pot, it was necessary to recite proper words to the Earth spirit. They honored the "Three Sisters," the spirits of their staple foods; corn, squash and beans.

Each tribe had shamans, priests or medicine men, who could interpret and intervene with spirits and determine ritual. The Indians were also

From a drawing made by Iroquois (about 1850) showing a dance ritual

superstitious, believing in what we call witchcraft.

Ceremonies and festivals were important. Each year there were at least six. The midwinter ceremony lasted for many days, a combination of ritual and fun. In the spring, thanks and prayers were given for the new season and for the rising of the maple syrup. Seeds were planted with prayers. There was also a midsummer festival and harvest ceremonies.

FALSE FACE SOCIETY

The Iroquois believed the woods were inhabited by evil beings who brought disease and misfortune to their people. Certain men of the tribe, they believed, gained powers to disperse such evils if they had a special type of dream. These men became members of the False Face Society. When there was illness in the tribe, one society member would go to the woods and select a tree.

With proper homage to the tree, he would carve a mask on the tree. The appropriate ceremony completed, the mask was cut away from the tree and painted red or black.

The masks had many expressions, always ugly, meant to frighten off the evil. Metal around the eyes created an eerie effect in the firelight. Masks were stored in special bags and treated like living things, sometimes given tobacco or food.

In the village, the mask was worn at special rituals. Fires were put out for the smoke to rise as a message to the gods. The masked dancer would go about, shaking a turtleshell rattle. During the dance, a handful of ashes were blown over the sick person. The curved cheeks on the mask shown represent this act of blowing.

Instructions follow to make an ash-blowing false face mask to hang on your wall or to wear at an Indian dance performance.

False face dancer with turtle shell rattle

Maché Mask

MATERIALS: Large oval paper plate, two drinking cups (foam or paper), newspapers, lightweight card, wallpaper paste, aluminum foil pan, household cement, masking tape, string, red paint and brush, rope. Optional: Celluclay.

Use paper plate (platter) for base or cut an oval of corrugated card 10″ × 12″. Draw center lines, draw and cut eyes and nose hole as shown (Fig. 1). Cut a nose

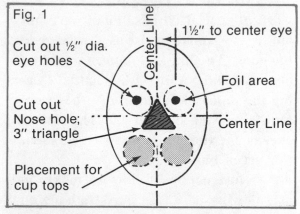

shape out of lightweight card (Fig. 2). Fold (Fig. 3). Tape nose on mask.

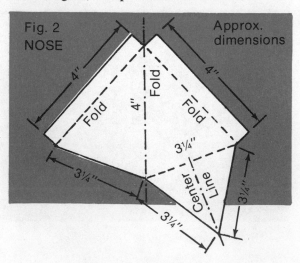

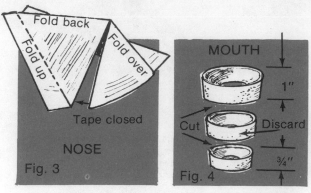

Cut top and base off two foam cups (Fig. 4) and tape tops in place (Fig. 5). Use the bottoms of the cups to form inside cheek areas. Cut a mouth slit between the cup rims (Fig. 6).

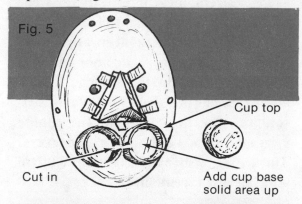

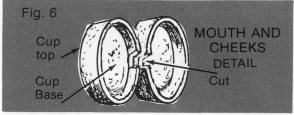

Prepare a thin solution of wallpaper paste. Tear strips of newspapers and soak in paste. Place strips, covering nose and mouth shapes. For a furrowed-brow look, use a full page of newspaper. Spread on paste and fold up into tight rolls. Add more paste and shape onto the mask (Fig. 7). Pinch off excess at edges. Add a roll of paper around the outside edge. A space about 3/4″ all around the eyes should be left flat. Place mask on a block or bowl. As it dries, shape edges down into mask contour (Fig. 8). Also shape features.

When dry, add a layer of smaller pieces (about 1″ × 2″) of paper soaked in the paste. Cover established shapes up over coils, around cups, etc. Accentuate all contours, furrows, lip, and cheek shapes. Allow to dry. If well formed, the mask is complete, although you might wish to refine the shapes with maché pulp (Celluclay). Prepare as directed, fill and shape as needed, emphasizing mouth and cheek shapes. Allow to dry. With an awl, punch three holes at the top and one on each side (see Fig. 5). Paint mask red.

Cut two 2″ circles of paper. Place on mask around eyes. Mark to fit flat area and trim. Once the shape is determined, cut out of aluminum foil plate. Cut eye holes. Using household cement, glue in place around eyes (Fig. 9).

Fig. 9

Aluminum Foil shape; glue on

Glue on

For hair, cut several pieces of rope about three feet long. Unravel. Insert string through each hole in top (Fig. 10) and tie around rope, attaching hanks to top of mask. Tie cords at each side to hold mask on head.

Fig. 10

Tie   Tie   Tie

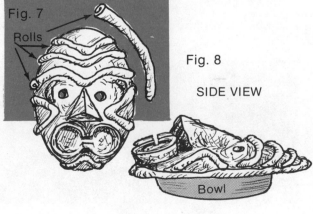

Fig. 7

Rolls

Fig. 8

SIDE VIEW

Bowl

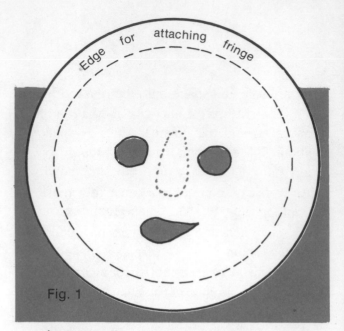

Fig. 1

ALTERNATE: For a more authentic look, use horsehair (instead of rope), available from Indian craft suppliers. (See back of book.)

Use your own ideas. What shape do you think most ugly for a false face mask to scare away evil spirits?

HUSK FACE MASK

Corn was an important food staple, especially to the Iroquois. At planting time there was a ceremony to insure a good harvest. Four kernels were planted in each hole as a token of respect for the four directions. In midsummer when the first green ears appeared on the stalks there was another celebration.

While not as powerful as the False Face Society, the Husk Face Society (Bushyheads), had importance in certain rituals. These masks were worn for the corn harvest dance and during the midwinter ceremonies. A wearer of a husk face mask never spoke.

Miniature masks were also made. Such a piece was probably used as a talisman or charm.

Miniature Mask

MATERIALS: Dried corn husks, waxed paper, brown card (oaktag), paper clip, pins, scrap of corrugated board, cord (or string), needle and thread, weights, glue, masking tape.

Trace Fig. 1 on card. Place card on corrugated board and tape wax paper over everything to keep dry.

Soak husks in water; shake off excess water. To make nose, use husk about 3/4" wide. Fold it around paper clip several times (Fig. 2). Tie top, using another piece of husk. Leave ends sticking up (Fig. 3). Ends of tie will start braid. Split long end in half and work in new husk for third strand. All braiding strips should be about 1/4" wide.

Pin nose in position over card shape, right side down. Start braiding, adding in new pieces as necessary (Fig.

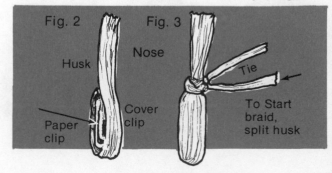

Fig. 2

Fig. 3

Nose

Husk

Cover clip

Paper clip

Tie

To Start braid, split husk

76

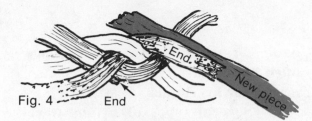

Fig. 4   End   End   New piece

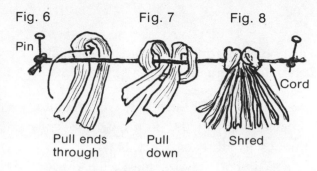

Fig. 6   Fig. 7   Fig. 8

Pin

Pull ends   Pull   Shred   Cord
through   down

4). If ends of new pieces stick out a bit, they can be trimmed later. The face can be one continuous braid. Braid, then coil around and pin (Fig. 5). Pin coils so that they lay flat against each other. Leave openings at eyes and mouth. Allow to dry somewhat, until braided coils begin to hold their shape.

While still damp, thread a needle and sew back and forth between coils, holding them flat. Only a little sewing is necessary—just enough so that mask can be picked up. Add a little glue if needed to hold. Remove mask and waxed paper, turn over, and lay on the card shape. Adjust outlines drawn on card to fit braided shape if it is now somewhat different. There should be 1/4″ extra all around for attaching fringe. Remove mask and cut out the card shape. Cut holes for eyes (a paper punch may do) and mouth.

To make fringe for edge, cut a piece of cord about 14″ long. Tie cord to pins. Cut a piece of wet husk about 1/2″ wide and at least 5″ long. Fold in half and loop over cord (Fig. 6). Tuck ends up

through loop. Pull so that ends stick out (Fig. 7). Continue adding pieces in this manner. Tightly cover about 8″ of cord, enough to go around the mask. Using a pin or fingernail, split fringe husks into pieces 1/8″ wide or less (Fig. 8).

Glue fringe around outside edge of card and glue mask in place onto card. Lay piece of wax paper over and weight down. Allow to dry.

Trim edges of fringe even about 2″ out from mask (Fig. 9). Sew a hanging cord through card at the top. This amulet

Fig. 5

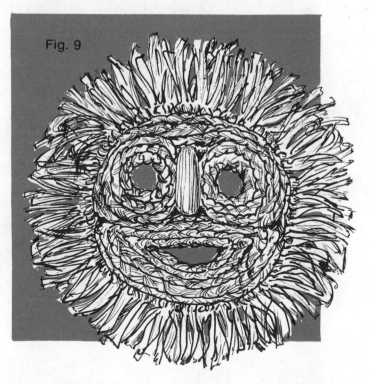

Fig. 9

can be hung from a belt or strap or makes an unusual ornament on a bulletin board.

ALTERNATES: Substitute raffia (natural or synthetic) for the corn husks. A continuous length is easier to braid.

For a full-size mask, the process would be much the same. For nose, start with dried corncob with husks attached (Fig. 10). Make larger, thicker braids. A

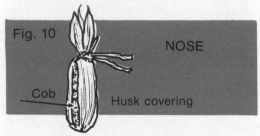

Fig. 10
NOSE
Cob
Husk covering

separate braid could be made around each eye and the mouth area. Mount on a paper plate (see previous mask project). Make a thick fringe, possibly a double layer, and sew around the outside.

RATTLES
AND OTHER MUSIC

Sounds and rhythms to accompany ceremonies and dances were created with drums, rattles, flutes, notched sticks, or objects jingled together. Most dances and songs were not merely entertainment but also had special significance. War dances worked up the emotions necessary to go to battle. Drumbeats and repetitive songs often had the hypnotic effect a shaman needed for his rituals.

Several types of drums were used by Woodland Indians. The Iroquois hollowed out a log, partly filled it with water. By varying the amount of water, tone was controlled. The Chippewa ceremonial drum was large, suspended on poles. Smaller hand drums, used by most tribes, had a rawhide head on one or sometimes both sides. They played with a stick, never using their hands to touch the drum.

Rattles were made of gourds, turtle shells, horn or dewclaws hung from a stick. Jingling cones, dewclaws or small turtle shells were hung from dancers' garters.

To get a good tone, a drum must be made of proper materials (available from Indian craft suppliers listed in back of book), but a rattle made of discarded materials can look and sound authentic.

Drums and Rattles

Gourd-Type Rattle

MATERIALS: Egg-shaped plastic container (from panty hose), tan felt, 12″ stick or dowel 1/2″ in diameter, nail, fabric, yarn or fur, beads or feathers, gravel or dried peas, thread and needle, hammer, coping saw, tape.

Separate the two halves and place a handful of gravel inside. Close egg and shake. When you are satisfied with the sound, set aside the gravel you'll be using. In center top (smaller half), hammer in a nail. Cut hole in the lower half using the coping saw. It does not have to be neat, just big enough for the stick to fit through (Fig. 1). Insert stick through bottom hole, up to top. Hammer nail into top of stick (Fig. 2). Insert gravel and close sections together. Tape at base, if necessary, to keep gravel from coming out.

Trace oval (Fig. 3) and cut two out of felt. Sew the two sections together around and covering the egg shape (Fig. 4). Sew sections closed at base and tie. Cut a piece of cloth about 1½″ × 18″. Sew or glue around egg base (Fig. 5), then

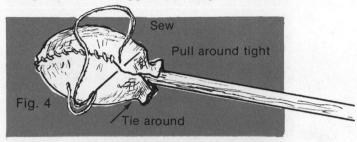

Fig. 4
Sew
Pull around tight
Tie around

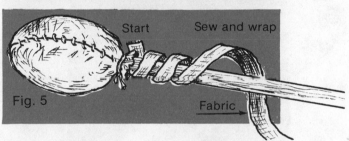

Fig. 5
Start
Sew and wrap
Fabric

wind around, covering the stick. Sew or glue end.

A decoration about 6″ or 8″ long should hang from the end. Make of yarn,

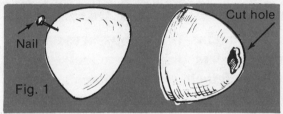

Nail
Cut hole
Fig. 1

Insert Gravel
Hole
Stick
Fig. 2

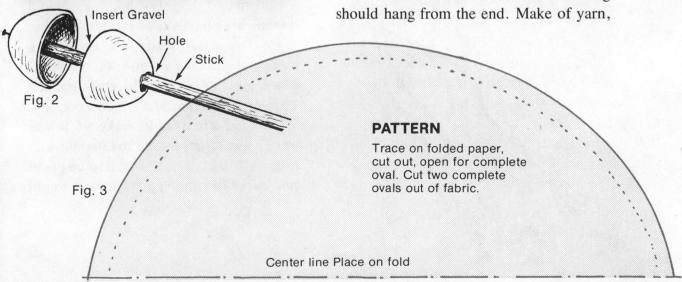

Fig. 3

PATTERN
Trace on folded paper, cut out, open for complete oval. Cut two complete ovals out of fabric.

Center line Place on fold

several strands sewn to end of fabric (Fig. 6). Glue and tie beads or feathers on ends, or use raveled rope. The Indian used horse or moose hair. Or sew on a piece of fake fur about 1″ wide.

ALTERNATES: For a more authentic look, cover egg with chamois. Cut two ovals 1/4″ less all around than felt, as chamois stretches. Wet chamois and sew around shape. Allow to dry.

If a gourd is available, make in similar manner, putting gravel into bottom hole before inserting stick. Then cover.

MAGIC, CHARMS AND FETISHES

The Midewiwin Society was an important part of the Chippewa's life. A boy who was to become a shaman had to study for a long time to memorize all the necessary rituals. To help him remember, he would write key pictures on birchbark scrolls to remind him of the chants. Once he had the knowledge, he was initiated into the society in a solemn and dramatic ceremony.

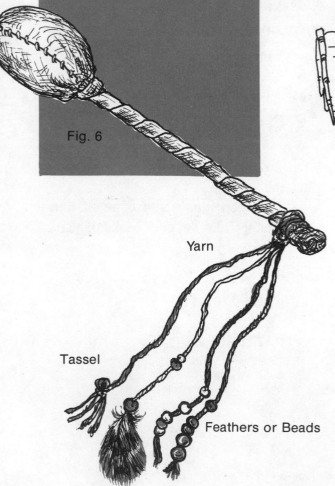

Fig. 6

Yarn

Tassel

Feathers or Beads

Mide Scroll

Shamans in various areas used many devices and tricks to impress the tribe with their powers. Some were jugglers or ventriloquists. Others used hypotism and sleight-of-hand. Each had a medicine bundle made of animal skin or an elaborately beaded bag containing objects such as claws, powdered insects, roots, and bones. The objects in the bag were often determined by dreams.

A shaman could make a fetish to insure good fortune for the person who needed it. But the fetish had to be properly cared for and renewed, or it would

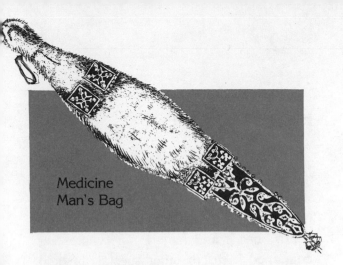

Medicine Man's Bag

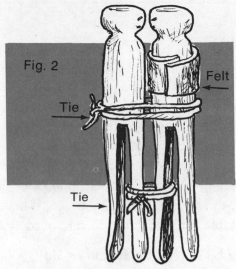

Fig. 2

Tie

Felt

Tie

lose its powers and become only an ornament, or talisman. It could be loaned, bought or inherited.

In some tribes, a girl who wished to win a certain man for her husband might have asked the shaman for a fetish. Some part of the desired person's body (nail or hair clipping) was placed between two crudely carved wooden dolls. With proper magic, the dolls were wrapped and tied together.

Charms are fun to make even if magic is no longer believed.

Love Fetish

MATERIALS: Two straight clothespins, scraps of felt, fake fur or fabric (preferably tan and browns), string (cord or yarn), beads, nylon line or thread, glue, small feather, felt-tipped markers or beads.

With black marker, draw dots for eyes and mouth on each clothespin (Fig. 1). Wrap a small piece of felt around one

clothespin and glue end. Tie the two together as shown (Fig. 2). Glue or sew on other pieces of fabric. Approximate sizes are shown in Fig. 3. Make edges raggedy or fringed for more authentic effect. The last and largest piece should have some

Fig. 3

Fuzzy fabric 4¼" x 1" Glue on

Beaded panel (or other decoration)

Felt or fabric 5" x 2¼"

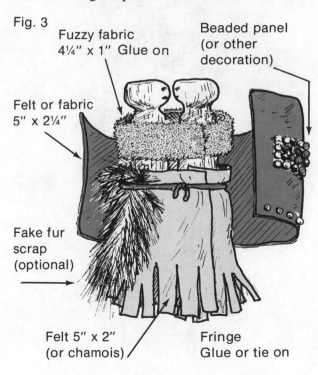

Fake fur scrap (optional)

Felt 5" x 2" (or chamois)

Fringe Glue or tie on

Fig. 1

decoration—embroidery or beadwork (see Chapter 4). Tiny dots could be added with colored markers for a beaded effect. Wrap fabric around and tie in several places with yarn and string.

Make a string of various size beads about 8″ long. Wrap around twice and tie. Sew or glue to hold in place, if necessary. Glue a tiny feather to one head (Fig. 4).

ALTERNATES: Carve dolls out of a piece of 3/4″ balsa about 4″ long by 3/4″ wide. Instead of felt use a leather scrap or chamois which makes a better fringe.

Fig. 4

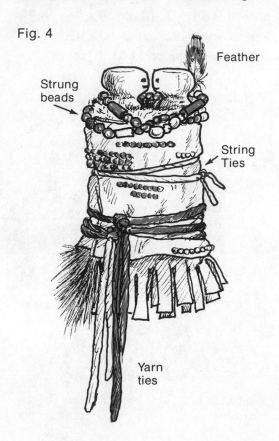

Feather

Strung beads

String Ties

Yarn ties

Health Charm

This charm was worn to insure good health. The design, such as the bear shown, probably represented a totem animal. Small shells were sewn behind the hands, head, and feet. Possibly the bag contained herbs or other special magical materials.

MATERIALS: Black felt or velvet, seed beads (white and one color), nylon line, needle and thread, black cord or narrow ribbon.

Cut a piece of felt about 3½″ × 8″. On paper, draw an area 3¼″ × 2½″. Inside this area drawn an outline of an animal (Fig. 1) or person (Fig. 2). For proper magic you should draw your own, not trace it. If you recently dreamed of an animal, real or imaginary, make it your totem. Transfer design to the felt and bead outline

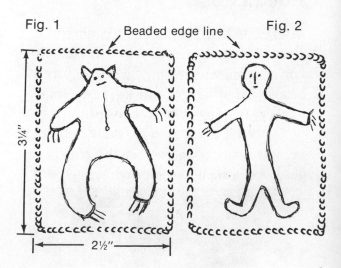

Fig. 1   Beaded edge line   Fig. 2

3¼″

2½″

in white (see page 70). Bead a colored row inside the white outline. Sew on beads for eyes and mouth. Bead a white outline along edge line.

Fold in half, wrong sides together, and sew sides of bag (Fig. 3). Turn right

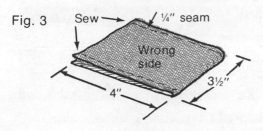

Fig. 3

Sew →

¼" seam

Wrong side

4"

3½"

side out. Sew on a cord or braided yarn. Hang around your neck or from a belt (Fig. 4).

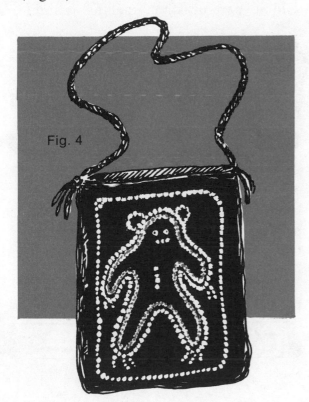

Fig. 4

TOBACCO AND PIPES

A bit of ground tobacco tossed in a fire created a fragrant smoke and rose to the skies as a message to the gods. By drawing the smoke through a tube, a person participated in the message to the powers above. The Indians also believed that smoke made a man think more clearly.

The long-stemmed pipe called a calumet was a sacred instrument, smoked only in solemn ceremonies. Smoking a calumet compelled a man to keep his pledge of honor and so was important to seal treaties and insure brotherhood.

The calumet was kept in a decorated buckskin bag and a special guard assigned to watch over it.

The stem of the pipe was often painted with sacred designs, such as symbols of the sky, and wrapped with

Calumet

Winebago Pipe; Catlinite bowl is inlaid with lead.

leather thongs, beads, quillwork or fur and feathers. Pipe bowls were made of clay or carved of stone. The Chippewas quarried black stone in Wisconsin. Other tribes used catlinite, found in areas west of Lake Superior that were considered sacred—no one tribe could own them.

Not all pipes were sacred; some tribes made pipes for personal use. The Europeans had no knowledge of tobacco or smoking until they met the Indians. Yet, within 100 years after the first explorers came, the entire continent of Europe was using tobacco.

Eventually some calumets were made without smoke holes, and were used merely as a decorative symbol of brotherhood.

Here's how to make a miniature symbolic pipe.

Miniature Peace Pipe

MATERIALS: Spool, wooden paint stirrer from hardware or paint store, dark red and brown paint, small and medium size brushes, yarn or other trim, glue, coping saw, sandpaper.

The shape of the paint stirrer is a good start to make a model of a calumet (less than 1/2 the size of the real one). With a coping saw, trim the stirrer, removing small, dark areas shown in Fig. 1. Sand and smooth edges. For bowl, use a

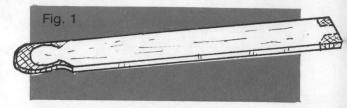

Fig. 1

small spool from sewing thread. Trim off upper flange (Fig. 2) and sand smooth. Paint spool dark red, and also paint ends of the stick (Fig. 3).

Thin the brown paint and stain middle part of stick, making it light

Fig. 2

Remove flange

Fig. 3

brown. With a small brush and brown paint, add designs as desired (Fig. 4). Glue spool to end. Glue and tie on yarn (Fig. 5).

Fig. 4

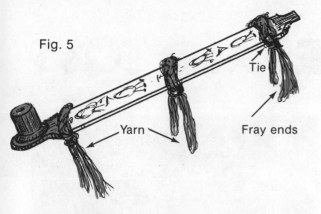

Fig. 5

Tie

Yarn

Fray ends

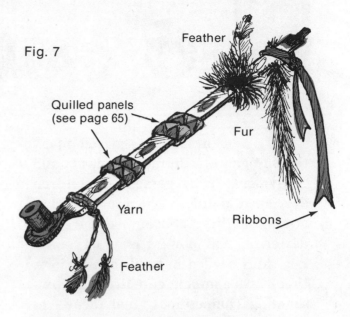

Fig. 7

Feather

Quilled panels
(see page 65)

Fur

Yarn

Ribbons

Feather

ALTERNATES: If you have and know how to use a woodburning tool, it is a good way to add the decorations. Burn edges slightly also (Fig. 6).

Trimmings can be as elaborate as desired. Instead of a painted design, cover sections with beaded panels. Or the entire stem can be wrapped with raffia, beadwork, or leather strips. Tuck feathers in

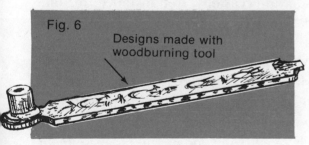

Fig. 6

Designs made with
woodburning tool

wrappings or hang from cords. If you can find some old fur tails, tack to pipe (Fig. 7).

For those who do woodworking, cut and shape a piece of wood. Those who do ceramics can make a bowl in the form

of an animal head (Fig. 8) like an Iroquois pipe. Attach bowl to wood stem.

Fig. 8

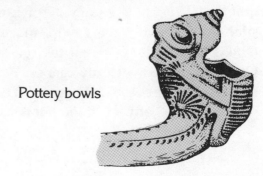

Pottery bowls

6 GAMES AND TOYS

The Indians played many types of games with much intensity and enjoyment. Most games for children developed abilities needed to survive as adults: agility, courage, endurance, dexterity, and powers of observation. For skills needed in battle as warriors, there were mock conflicts, arrow-shooting competitions, and throws at targets, both moving and stationary. In one game, a team would roll small hoops and the other team would try to throw spears through. There were running, hopping, and jumping races, tug-of-war, and wrestling. Follow-the-leader through the woods taught observation skills. The leader might imitate birds and animals, making sounds for the boys to identify. Blindfolded in the center of a circle, a child developed acute hearing as another player tried to get close enough to touch him. This second player was learning how to stalk quietly. They had games of pick-up-sticks, corn cob darts, tops, marbles (small round stones), and toss games. Children played with toy canoes, floating ducks, and toy toboggans. Dolls were made of any available materials:

Doll and duck of cattail reeds. Pine needle doll was placed on bark and shaken to make doll "dance."

pine needles, reeds, corn husks, leather scraps.

Adults also played games, many of which had ceremonial purposes for special occasions. For instance, for one ceremony, two teams sat on either side of a board with referees watching. Musicians and singers accompanied the ritual. A small stone was handed to one team and passed from hand to hand, up and down the row. When the music changed, someone of the opposite team had to guess which hand held the stone.

There were many guessing games, as well as games of chance, played at festivals. Such games continued for days and often included betting. Losers might forfeit all they owned.

Both men and women played team sports. Often a whole tribe—hundreds of people—would participate. A variety of ballgames were played with several to many players. The balls were made of buckskin with clay or sand filling. Lacross and hockey developed from the Indian games, only now the number of players is limited.

In all games, competition was strong. To be injured was considered a disgrace, yet games were very rough and many did get injured. When hurt, a boy might sneak away, hoping his friends would not notice. Back home, his grandmother might apply herbs for healing and possibly bind the wound with a corn husk bandage.

A few games are suggested below, some from adult, others from children's games.

GAMES TO MAKE AND PLAY

MATERIALS: (depending on the game) Dowels or sticks, paints, feathers, yarn, glue, tape, weight, corncob, saw, awl, knife, or chalk.

Flip Stick

Cut a 1/2″ stick or dowel about three feet long. Paint stripes on one end. Make a mark on the ground. Hold stick as

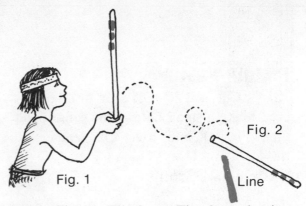

Fig. 1   Fig. 2   Line

shown (Fig. 1). Flip it up (Fig. 2) so that it lands over the line. Before each flip, predict how you intend it to land: stripe end away or toward you. Opponents give their guess—on the line or sideways, perhaps. After it lands, give points to the one who predicted right. It's wise to practice before competing.

Guess Sticks

Cut two identical dowels or sticks about 10″ long. Paint or make a small cut mark on the end of one stick. Sit on the floor opposite your opponent with hands behind your back. Shift sticks with hand over marked end (Fig. 3). Bring hands to front so opponent can guess which hand has the stick with the mark. The Indians enjoyed the bluffing in this game.

Fig. 3

Paddle Feathers

Cut a 1½"-piece of dried corn-cob. Make a small hole in the center, add glue (Fig. 4), and insert four feathers 3" or 4" long. Use a wooden paddle to knock it back and forth between players, like badminton.

Fig. 4
Feathers
Corn cob

Weighted Feather

Select a large feather about 12" long, and a small fishing weight with a groove (Fig. 5). If necessary, whittle the lead a bit to accommodate the tip of the feather. With household cement, glue the tip into the weight. Add tape around to secure (Fig. 6). Each player makes his own weighted feather. Add a different color on each feather with felt markers, if needed for identification. Scratch a small circle in the ground or chalk a circle on the sidewalk. Determine a line to throw from. Toss the feather, trying to get the weighted tip in the circle. Wind and flight angles add interest here.

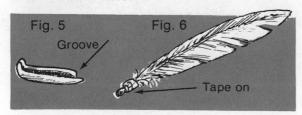

Fig. 5
Groove
Fig. 6
Tape on

Bowl Toss

Use six clean peach pits or similar shaped objects. Paint a spot on one side of each pit (Fig. 7). Place pits in a large, flat wooden bowl. For scoring, use beans, as the Indians did (or buttons or pennies), as counters.

Fig. 7
Fig. 8

Teams of about three players each sit facing each other. The first player shakes the bowl, then hits bowl down hard on the floor or table, sending pits in air (Fig. 8). How they land back in the bowl determines the score. The player then takes number of beans equal to score. See scoring chart (Fig. 9). Then next player shakes the bowl. Continue around, then count up beans (points) for each team and repeat as often as you want. The Indians played for days at a time.

Fig. 9	SCORING CHART	
Six of same (blanks or spots)		10
Five of same		5
Four of same		2
Three of same		2

WINTER GAMES

Many outdoor games were played in winter; it was a good way to get out of a cramped, smoky house and take some rugged exercise. Team games on ice were popular.

A skill game, with much betting on the winner, was the Snow Snake, played by the strongest men of the tribe. A stick, the "snake," often as long as ten feet, was slid along a snow trench or over ice. Stories around the Great Lakes tell of a warrior who hurled his snake a mile.

Snakes were carefully shaped, polished, and greased. The medicine man might have even added a special potion to make it perform better. Preparing the groove took much time and proper snow conditions. After a throw, a marker was put at the farthest distance reached, and others tried to exceed it. Undoubtedly, young boys practiced the game using smaller snow snakes. If you live in an area that has snow, try a small version.

Snow Snake

MATERIALS: Quarter round molding (harder, heavier wood is preferable), log and cord, saw, plane or whittling knife, two screws, two nuts, sealer such as varnish or acrylic polymer medium, wax, screwdriver, sandpaper, stain, or paint brush. Optional: sticks about 12″ long, yarn.

Obtain molding from lumber yard, and cut a piece about 4′ long. Rounded side is the bottom. Plane or whittle a flat area (Fig. 1) for back of snake. Leave top of head with angled shape (Fig. 2). Whittle base and tip, shaping head as shown. Smooth, first with rough, then with fine sandpaper. Paint with thinned paint or stain and allow to dry. Paint a design on the back (Fig. 3) if desired. When dry, apply the sealer.

Mark spots for eyes (Fig. 4). Poke holes with awl and slide screw through nut

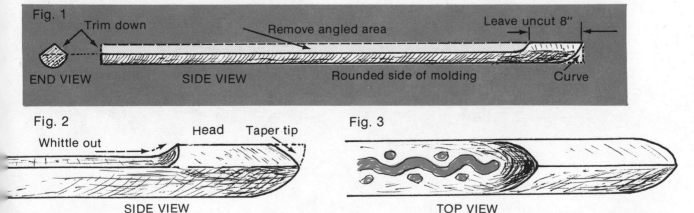

Fig. 1
Trim down   Remove angled area   Leave uncut 8″
END VIEW   SIDE VIEW   Rounded side of molding   Curve

Fig. 2
Whittle out   Head   Taper tip
SIDE VIEW

Fig. 3
TOP VIEW

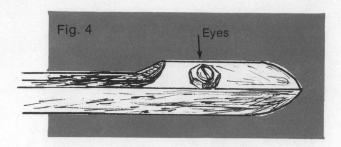
Fig. 4

Eyes

(Fig. 5), then screw into head (Fig. 6). Although screws give the look of eyes, they are primarily for weight at the front. Cover snake with several coats of paste-wax and rub thoroughly.

Fig. 5

Screw

Nut

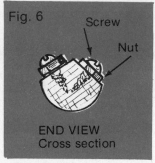
Fig. 6

Screw

Nut

END VIEW
Cross section

If desired, make markers. Tie yarn or feathers onto a stick (Fig. 7). Make a different color marker for each player.

To prepare the groove, select a day with good, fresh snow on the ground about the right consistency for making snow-men. Tie a cord or rope on a fireplace log. Drag the log in a straight line through the snow in a level area (Fig. 8). The groove should be quite long, possibly across a ball field. Test a few throws, then pack and smooth the groove wherever needed.

To make snake travel as far as possible, it should be slid, not thrown. Each player takes turns sliding the snake and places a marker where his snake stopped.

If your groove is short, the winner can be determined by the one who slides his snake the entire length the most times.

Perhaps you could utilize modern devices for groove. If you can find an un-used parking lot, such as at school on a weekend, covered with new snow, have someone drive a car in a straight line across the lot. Although tire tracks make too wide a channel, it is well-packed. It is a quick way to get started playing the game.

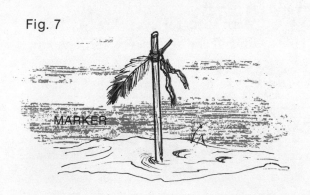
Fig. 7

MARKER

Fig. 8

ALTERNATE: If you have limited space or no flat areas, try canoe sliding, another Indian version of the game. Cut a 16"-piece of the quarter-round molding (Fig. 9). Whittle, carve, or file into the shape

Fig. 9

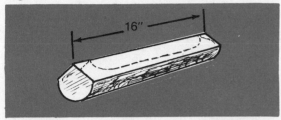

shown (Fig. 10). Finish as before. Add a lead fishing weight in front if necessary. Each player can have a canoe and make his own channel on a slope or hill. Place

Fig. 10

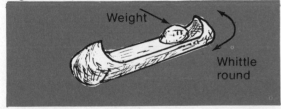

Weight

Whittle round

canoes at the top. At the shout of "go," each gives his canoe a shove to slide it down the hill. The first one at the bottom wins. With one channel and one canoe, see who can slide the canoe farthest.

DOUBLE BALL GAME

This game was played by women with unlimited numbers on each side. The double ball was tossed in the middle of a field with goalposts on each end. Sticks were used to lift, toss, or carry the ball, attempting to get it hung over the goal.

This game is much too dangerous for today when we are concerned about the safety of players. However, the double ball is interesting to make. With new rules that keep opponents far enough apart, there is little chance of harm.

MATERIALS: Four plastic practice golf balls from a sporting goods store, chamois, leather boot lacing at least 18" long, buttonhole thread and needle, sandpaper, knife, two sticks. Optional: fishing weights, goal sticks.

You can buy boot lacing (rawhide) from most shoe repair shops or 1/8" thong from a craft store. It *must* be strong. Slide two of the plastic balls onto the thong and knot the end (Fig. 1), leaving about 3" at

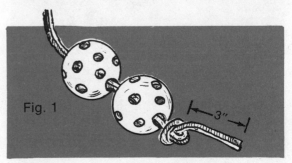

Fig. 1

3"

the end. Cut two 5″ squares from the chamois or leather. Cut corners slightly round (Fig. 2). Wet chamois, curve, and stretch around both balls, holding balls to-

Fig. 2

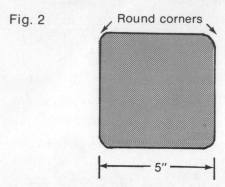

Round corners

5″

gether. Sew sides (Fig. 3), gather end (Fig. 4), and pull up tight around balls (Fig. 5). Repeat on other end. Wrap thread around gathers and knot. Wrap another piece of thread several times around the middle between balls, pull tight, and knot.

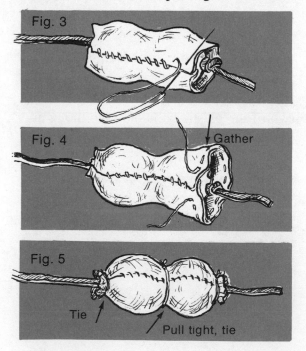

Fig. 3

Fig. 4
Gather

Fig. 5
Tie
Pull tight, tie

Slide the other two balls on the thong and knot end, leaving about 8″ of thong between center balls, 3″ at the end. Trim. Cover this pair of balls the same as the first two. If you have some scrap pieces of thong, cut two 5″ pieces for decoration. Tie another knot in thong at one end, slide piece inside (Fig. 6) and tighten

Fig. 6

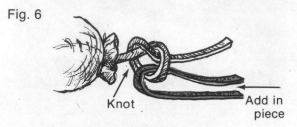

Knot
Add in piece

knot. Wetting will make knot tighter. Repeat on other end (Fig. 7).

ALTERNATES: Ball covering can be felt or any sturdy fabric, but leather is the most durable. If using fabric, cut squares 5½″.

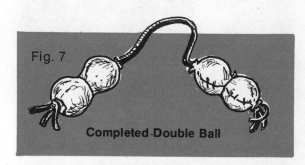

Fig. 7
Completed Double Ball

Added weight can make the balls toss better. Fishing weights, split shot sinkers #5, will fit through the holes in the balls. Insert three or four before covering.

TO PLAY: A tossing stick about three feet long is needed. Find a dead branch with a curve at the end (Fig. 8). Remove bark. Sand and whittle end to shape. Try tossing and catching the double ball by its thong middle. Players can take turns to see who does it best. It's tricky and takes practice.

Each player has a playing stick. He tosses the ball over the goalpost to his opponent, who must catch it with his stick (Fig. 9), then try to flip the ball back, onto the crossbar of the goal (Fig. 10). Determine the point value of a catch and for scoring a goal.

Fig. 10

SCORE!

Fig. 8

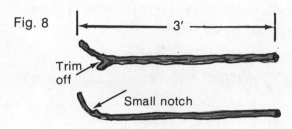

Trim off

Small notch

For a game for two, set up a goal post. The height of the crosspiece should be about eye level. A badminton or volley ball net can be used, but a stick is better.

Fig. 9

Goal posts set in ground, cross piece lashed (or nailed) across.

SOURCES OF SUPPLY

Local crafts, hobby, or art stores have most materials that are needed to make the projects in this book. For mail order suppliers, write first to inquire about the charge for their catalog. Most carry beads, cords, and glues.

AMERICAN HANDICRAFTS CO. (TANDY LEATHER) (Stores nationwide).
Look in your local phone book for address or write: 1001 Foch Street, Fort Worth, TX 76107

ARTIS, INC., Box A, Solvang, CA 93463
Bow Loom, Swisstraw.

H.H. PERKINS CO., 10 South Bradley Road, Woodbridge, CT 06525
Round reed, wood and fiber splints.

NASCO ART AND CRAFTS, 901 Janesville Avenue, Fort Atkinson, WI 53538.
General art and craft materials of all kinds.

The following suppliers carry a full line of Indian craft materials: various size feathers, horsehair, fur, shells, imitation beadwork, drum kits, suedecloth fabric, special beads, etc:

GREY OWL INDIAN CRAFT CO. INC., 150-02 Beaver Road, Jamaica, NY 11433

PLUME TRADING AND SALES CO. INC., P.O. Box 585, Monroe, NY 10950

SUPERNAW'S OKLAHOMA INDIAN SUPPLY, Box 216 Skiatook, OK 74072

INDEX